essent

M AGING
YO DEBT

"If you are finding it difficult keeping on top of your mortgage payments, credit cards and loans, then this book is for you. If you are so overstretched you don't know how you will carry on making repayments, this book will guide you through the maze of rules that can, in the worst cases, lead to bankruptcy. **"**

Phillip Inman

About the author

Phillip Inman has been a journalist for 18 years specialising in personal finance and business. For the last nine years he has worked for the *Guardian* newspaper and has written extensively about unfair practices in the financial services industry and the nation's growing problem with debt.

MANAGING YOUR DEBT

PHILLIP INMAN

This book is dedicated to my wife Kendra
and my children Miranda, Joseph and Olivia

Which? Books are commissioned and published by Which? Ltd,
2 Marylebone Road, London NW1 4DF
Head of Which? Books: Angela Newton
Project management for Which? Books: Luke Block
Email: books@which.co.uk

Distributed by Littlehampton Book Services Ltd, Faraday Close, Durrington, Worthing,
West Sussex BN13 3RB

British Library Cataloguing in Publication Data
A catalogue record for this book is available from the British Library

Author's acknowledgements
I'd like to thank Emma Callery for her patience and eye for detail. I also want to thank
Luke Block and Angela Newton at Which?, Lisa Taylor at Moneyfacts, Gillian Key-Vice at
Experian, Neil Munro at Equifax, Jane Bellis at the Consumer Credit Counselling Service
and Sarah Miller at the Citizens Advice Bureau.

The publishers would like to thank Martyn Saville at Which? for his comments on the
manuscript.

Edited by: Emma Callery
Designed by: Bob Vickers
Index by: Lynda Swindells
Cover photographs by: Alamy
Printed and bound by Scotprint, Scotland

FSC
Mixed Sources
Product group from well-managed
forests and other controlled sources
Cert no. TT-COC-2217
www.fsc.org
© 1996 Forest Stewardship Council

For a full list of Which? Books, please call 01903 828557, access our website at
www.which.co.uk, or write to Littlehampton Book Services.
For other enquiries call 0800 252 100.

Contents

Introduction

Much of what we buy, from our first car to a college education, is funded by debt. When we're in control, it allows us to buy a house, take a holiday or refashion a kitchen. Without access to credit, we would be forced to save over many years for most of the important things we need in life.

While there are people who think that switching to a culture of saving would make for a better world, most people have little choice but to borrow money if they are going to get ahead.

In answer to this demand, banks and other lenders sell hundreds of different types of loans. From the 50-day free loan period on a credit card to a 25-year mortgage, the range is vast. Just a short trip down the high street offers a rich choice of financial products. Log on to the internet and there will be hundreds more. They are not hard to find. Finance companies advertising loans large and small, long and short appear on radio and TV, newspapers and billboards, often with a famous face urging us to spend money using one of their loans.

> **❝** While there are those who argue that a saving culture would make the world better, most of us have little choice but to borrow money. **❞**

Borrowing statistics

Most of us have said yes to one type of loan or another, which is how the proportion of households with unsecured debt has increased from 36 per cent to 43 per cent since 1995. Personal borrowing in Britain reached £1.2 trillion in 2006, with almost £220 billion of it in unsecured loans.

BUYING A DREAM

For many, debt worries are about stretching credit limits to get a bigger house or better car. We fret about getting the best deal – the cheapest interest rate, avoiding penalties and minimising the amount of small print. But we fail to ask ourselves whether we are over-extended and if we could get in to trouble if the worst happens and we lose our job or fall ill, or interest rates rise. And even if we do ask the difficult questions about our personal finances, most of us shy away from making the hard choices. We take out the loan and hope for the best. We don't read the small print or listen carefully when the sales pitch is in full swing.

If the monthly direct debt sounds affordable, we sign on the dotted line. A more rigorous analysis of the deal might have revealed it was overambitious and left us over extended, but that would mean saying 'no' to the bank's advances and realising we could not afford our dream. Some people let the bank decide. If it allows you to keep spending, then it must think you can afford it.

LETTING DEBTS SLIP

Most people get away with taking this attitude. They don't lose their job, fall ill or get divorced. They can afford the monthly repayments and have little problem dealing with their lenders.

However, a growing number are struggling to cope. Analysts at one City investment bank have estimated that up to two million of us are close to losing control of our debts. That's ten times the official Bank of England estimate of 200,000. It only takes for mortgage interest rates to increase or, as we saw in 2006, for energy prices to rise by a third, for households to reach for a loan or credit card to maintain their living standard.

Families can easily find themselves overwhelmed as they struggle to pay for school trips and holidays along with clothes, petrol and food. They will ask if extending their mortgage is the best way to see them through a bad patch? Should several loans be consolidated into one super loan, and should free interest periods on a credit card be spurned in favour of a secured loan? This book helps you if you are struggling to see your way through the financial maze. It also tells you how to handle the situation if you are truly broke and need to take more drastic action.

> **"** Families can find themselves overwhelmed as they struggle to pay for school trips and holidays along with clothes and food. **"**

THE END OF CHEAP MONEY

Last year, more than 100,000 people applied to go **bankrupt** or for an **individual voluntary arrangement** (IVA) to repay their debts. Many economists believe the situation is going to get worse over the next few years. A decade of cheap money is coming to an end, they argue, and we are entering an era of higher interest rates and therefore higher debt repayments. Few predict a return to the soaring interest rates of the late 1980s and the full-scale recession that followed, but most acknowledge that we will probably pay more to maintain our debts over the next few years.

Many of the things people like to buy – houses, conservatories, new kitchens – have gone up in price, meaning that you need to take out a bigger loan to step up the housing ladder or improve your home. Furthermore, the demand for housing has resulted in the cost of buying a home doubling in most areas over the last ten years, and even trebling in places such as London.

While some predict a house price crash to bring the price tag of a home more in line with incomes, the chronic shortage, especially of family homes, looks like pushing prices ever higher. That means even bigger mortgages and larger debts.

WHO IS MOST IN DEBT?

Recent studies have shown that the group up to their eyes in debt are in their early thirties. These people are buying homes and furnishing them at a time when house prices have never been higher relative to household incomes. That means they are stretching the amount of money they borrow to the limit. Known to some banks as the 'Friends' generation after the popular US sitcom, this group not only have large mortgages, they also have the most debt on credit cards and unsecured loans. To make matters worse, they are the most likely to miss monthly repayments and incur penalty charges.

Another group near the edge of insolvency are in their mid thirties. They are single and rent their homes. They owe more than their annual income in unsecured debts (108 per cent on average). Over half of them have no savings at all. Overall, they make up less than 5 per cent of households, but their position is the most precarious. The **Consumer Credit Counselling Service** (CCCS) says the majority of people it sees in this situation are women.

These are not the only people who are in debt. The studies also reveal that the number of over forties seeking help has caught up with the thirtysomethings. Official figures show that almost six out of every ten people in their forties are paying off mortgages or some other debt. Equally, there are plenty of other groups who have huge debts. College graduates leave higher education with an average £16,000 debt and that figure is expected to continue rising over the next few years. In chapter 3, we take a detailed look at student finance.

At the other end of the age scale, pensioners have been hit hard in recent years by rising fuel bills and soaring council tax. Like many other pensioner groups, retired homeowners, usually one of the more affluent sections of the community, have sought to maintain their standard of living using loans. When the loans become unaffordable, they are encouraged to sell part of their home using an **equity release scheme** and

To find out more about the Consumer Credit Counselling Service (CCCS), go to www.cccs.co.uk. For the Citizens Advice Bureau, go to www.adviceguide.org.uk and for Payplan, go to www.payplan.com or call 0800 917 7823.

Jargon buster

Bankrupt When you become insolvent and have no money to pay creditors, you may find the best course of action is to become bankrupt. It is a legal process that protects you from further claims by creditors. You can emerge from bankruptcy in one year or sometimes less. But all your main assets will be sold to pay debts and if you still have a decent income, you may be forced to make repayments for up to three years. You can borrow again after one year, but it is difficult to arrange without paying a high interest rate

Consumer Credit Counselling Service (CCCS) Free advice service founded in 1993 that has helped over one million people. It is supported by the major lenders who will often refer customers to CCCS advisers, especially when the customer has multiple debts. See also Citizens Advice and Payplan (pages 139-41)

Equity release scheme Sold by insurance companies, banks and building societies to mainly retired homeowners. One type

of scheme involves you selling a portion of your home in return for a cash lump sum. The other is a mortgage that releases cash, with the mortgage payments deducted from the house value when you die

Individual voluntary arrangement (IVA) A form of insolvency that stops short of bankruptcy. It is a legal contract between you and your creditors that allows you to pay them all or some of the debt owed. You must stick to the agreed monthly payments for up to five years while your creditors must agree not to harass you for more than the sum originally agreed. After the five years you are clear to borrow again

Payment protection policies Insurance policy designed to cover payments on credit cards, loans and mortgages. Huge drawbacks with these policies are rarely mentioned by lenders who make vast profits selling them. If you really need to cover your payments, opt for an income protection plan sold by an independent broker

often, part of the capital released is used to pay off debts. In pages 110–11 we examine equity release schemes as a route out of debt for retirees.

Then there are those people who rack up large debts after suffering huge upheaval in their domestic lives. They or their partner could have lost their job or suffered an accident, or they might have split with their partner and be getting divorced. Any shock like this can hurt personal finances and taking on debt can seem to be one way out.

❝ People of all ages, from graduates to pensioners, can find they need to take on a debt. ❞

LOSING CONTROL

If our lives take an unexpected turn and the debts pile up, we worry. We get stressed. Some of us feel guilty and blame ourselves. Others become angry and blame those around them. Meanwhile, overdrafts ratchet upwards and we take extra loans to consolidate or pay off old ones. Those in major debt fear the worst. Debt helplines say callers ask if they will lose their home or even be sent to prison and their children taken into care.

While you can't be sent to prison or lose your children because you are bankrupt, losing control of your finances can have terrible consequences. Home repossessions, for example, were at a ten-year high in 2006. Will we see a return to the early 1990s when tens of thousands of people lost their homes through repossession by lenders? Given how many people are at the limit of their credit, if today's lenders get tough on payment arrears, we could once again see many more people handing back their keys.

Renters also face a dire situation if they ignore their debts. Many believe new rules allowing speedy bankruptcies (discussed in chapter 6, see box, below) are the equivalent of a 'Get Out of Jail Free' card in Monopoly. But bankruptcy is by no means an easy option and can still leave you financially scarred.

❝ Losing control of your finances can have terrible consequences. For example, home repossessions reached a ten-year high in 2006. **❞**

 Chapter 6 considers how you set about dealing with insolvency (pages 144–6), then looks into specific ways to overcome your problems, ranging from applying for an IVA (pages 147–50) to using an IVA company (pages 151–3) or bankruptcy (pages 154–66).

GETTING A GRIP

Reading this book means you have begun the process of dealing with debt. But before drafting a battle plan, there are some basics about lenders and how they operate that you need to know before addressing each of your debts, whether it is your mortgage that is the chief worry, credit card debts or loans.

Understanding how the credit reference system works and how you can suffer from a poor credit rating is also a must before you begin tackling your debt, just as you need to understand the way that interest and penalty charges can knock your calculations unless you get them under control. Then you can write down a list of creditors and your debts and lay the groundwork for getting the best deal from each one.

Chapter 1 gives you the tools to judge the extent of your problem. Then Chapters 2, 3 and 4 tackle each type of debt. We approach each subject – credit cards, loans and mortgages – on the basis that the increasing cost of living means you want to get your debts under control and start the process of managing them in a more sophisticated way. This is precisely where this book can help you, whether you believe you have a small, isolated problem or something that is, in fact, much bigger.

"Before you can tackle your debt, you need to understand the credit reference system and the way interest and penalty charges work."

If the worst has happened and you can't meet repayments on loans, you can skip straight to Chapter 5, which tells you the rules and shows you how to negotiate with creditors (see pages 116–42). It also gives you the tools you need to work out a plan of action so that you can begin to settle your debts.

If your situation is even worse, there is the comparatively new IVA that sets up a formal repayment scheme with creditors (see pages 147–50). Criticism of the IVA (mainly its exorbitant cost) has led to changes that in 2008 will bring a simpler and cheaper version.

This book also shows you how to negotiate to stabilise your borrowing before it gets out of control and how to juggle your debts and maximise your spending power (see pages 116–23). For instance, we list the ten questions to ask every loan provider before signing up (see page 83). It might be a credit card or an unsecured loan, a car credit

 If your debt is out of control and you can't decide between the merits of applying for an IVA compared with becoming bankrupt, the pros and cons of each are given on pages 148 and 160.

scheme or store card. Whatever the type of credit, there are simple steps you can take to help avoid the worst offenders.

- **Banks and other finance companies** charge hefty fees for setting up loans and add huge penalties when we fail to follow the small print. These are costs you need to avoid as they can add hugely to your debts.
- **Insurance policies** sold with loans and credit cards are also to blame for adding to people's debts and should be challenged.
- **Sky high interest rates** on credit cards and bank overdrafts have been creeping up and adding to debt bills.

Lenders have catered for every kind of person and situation with their debt products. It is a bewildering array and can ensnare even the savvy borrower. Use this book to help you navigate your way around the system, whatever your situation.

❝The worst offenders are set-up and penalty fees, insurance policies sold with loans, and high credit card and overdraft interest rates.❞

Debt basics

This chapter helps you to start the process of getting back in control. When you realise debts are getting out of hand, it is easy to panic and the problem can seem overwhelming and even insurmountable. Instead of taking any action, you let the situation drift. Letters get left in a pile on a bedside table or stuffed unopened in a rack, waiting for the day you are brave enough to peek inside and see how much you have let things stack up.

1

Dealing with debt

The information in this section aims to give you the tools to start tackling your debt problems. They may be mild and just need a bit of tinkering to sort them out. They may be serious and put you on the edge of bankruptcy. Whichever situation applies to you, your debts need to be tackled because they won't go away.

Of course, the psychology, which is well known among debt advisers, can lead you into a negative spiral. You blame others for not intervening or blame the system for your ills. Whatever the reason, the result is inaction at the very moment when reacting to your changed circumstances can save a huge amount of money and grief later on. Start taking control with the following steps.

STEP 1: COMMUNICATE

The first thing to remember is not to panic. Recognise that you have a problem and try talking about your situation. Telling yourself and others that you are experiencing financial problems can be the starting point for resolving your various issues. If you owe a friend or relative money, then you should inform them that you are in financial difficulties, but haven't forgotten the debt you owe them.

STEP 2: ASSESS YOUR SITUATION

In the home as much as in business, debt management is rapidly becoming one of our chief preoccupations. The increasing use of loans, mortgages and credit cards to buy things means managing debts is an essential job that competes with watching our favourite TV shows and walking the dog during evenings and weekends. Knowing the figures for your income and basic outgoings are crucial in assessing where you stand.

- **Your income could be steady,** but your outgoings might have increased since you first took out loans or credit cards. Or maybe it is your income that has declined relative to your outgoings.
- **If you simply had a spending splurge** and are now finding it difficult to keep interest payments from adding up, you still need to start thinking about how much money you have spare each month.

Whatever the reasons for your mounting debts, you need to understand how much of your income is spent on essentials and how much is spent on things you could or should give up in order to put your life back on track. In that way, you will know what money is available for your battle plan. Start by assessing who you pay (or owe) money to each month, and how much.

- **Make a list of all the people and companies** that have lent you money (your creditors).
- **Gather together the latest statements** from your bank, loan company and credit card provider(s).
- **Check how much you owe utility companies** (gas/electricity/water) and your local council (council tax).

- **If you pay rent,** find out if you are behind with payments.
- **If you pay a mortgage,** also check if you are behind with payments.

You will need the following information for each debt:

- The name and address of the creditor
- The account or reference number
- The amount you owe.

It is useful to list them all in one place and along the lines of the different columns given below.

Creditor information

Creditor's name	Address	Account/reference number	Amount owed

Don't employ guesswork. The likelihood is that the situation has changed over recent months and the figures could be worse than you thought. If you can't find a document telling you how much an insurance policy costs each month or the latest credit card statement, ring up the appropriate organisation for an up-to-date figure. Ultimately, you need to be honest with yourself and make sure that the amounts are as close to reality as possible.

Prioritise your debts

Once you've made a list of all your creditors, you need to work out which ones to deal with first. Some debts are more important than others. The debts you deal with first are called 'priority debts'. Once these debts are sorted out, you can address your 'non-priority debts'. Examples of each are given on pages 18–19 and

❝ The fewer excuses you have to ignore bills and vital information, the better. Debts need to be 'in your face' for you to deal with them. ❞

Money management tips

- Keep the latest letter or statement for each debt together in one place so that you can find them if you need them. Putting them in a folder or ring binder is an effective way to store documents and gives you easy access. Don't put the folder at the back of a wardrobe or other out-of-the-way place. The fewer excuses you have to ignore bills or check vital information, the better. Debts need to be 'in your face' for you to deal with them. The best place to keep them is on an open shelf in the kitchen or other well-used room.

- If you've received any court papers or letters that demand payment and seem urgent, you may need to act quickly. If you are not sure from the papers what you should do next, get advice straight away from a financial or legal expert, many of whom give free advice (see pages 139–42).

throughout the book we explain how to deal with both types of debt.

Beware, that while you can't be sent to prison for your failure to pay non-priority debts, your creditors can make trouble for you. If you don't make any offers to pay, without explaining why, they may take you to court. If you still fail to pay when the court has ordered it, your creditors can then take further action. For example, they can get another court order, which allows them to send bailiffs round to your home. While bailiffs can't enter your home without your permission, their presence is a clear signal that you are close to the edge and in need of independent debt advice.

Jargon buster

Bailiff A person licensed to confiscate your property to pay a debt. Must have documents confirming their identity and that a court has sanctioned them to retrieve goods on behalf of one of your creditors. There are complicated rules about what they can take and how they can take it. If one appears at your door, refuse him or her entry and seek advice immediately

Civil court The High Court in London and county courts around the country hear civil cases. You won't have committed a criminal act by reneging on debts, so cases are not heard in magistrate or crown courts. A judge will hear the case, though most are uncontested and a formality. There are costs applied by the court that can be waived if you are on a low income

Secured loan A loan offered in return for security. Usually the security is a portion of your property. It could be your car or expensive jewellery, but it is rare that mainstream lenders will accept anything other than your home. If you already have a mortgage, then a secured loan will, in effect, be a second mortgage on your home. It will usually have a variable interest rate and run for anywhere between 10 and 30 years

Unsecured loan A loan offered without security. It is a contractual arrangement in which you agree to repay the loan. Lenders will make a judgement based on your credit rating and employment status and income. Usually a fixed interest rate applies. Such loans are commonly paid back over three or five years

 The rules covering bailiffs' powers are complex and have changed recently as a result of the new Companies Act. For more information about the bailiffs in England and Wales, see pages 172-5.

Priority debts

These debts include:

Mortgage or rent arrears

- If you don't pay these, you could be in default and lose your home.

Fuel arrears

- You could be disconnected if you fail to pay gas and electricity bills.

Council tax arrears

- A court can use bailiffs to take your goods if you fall behind on council tax payments. If you manage to avoid the bailiffs or still owe money after they have taken your worldly belongings, the council can apply to the criminal court and you can be sent to prison.

Court fines

- Court fines, such as magistrates' court fines for traffic offences. If you don't pay these, the court can, again, use bailiffs and threaten prison.

Maintenance arrears

- Maintenance arrears payable to an ex-partner or children. This includes any child support you owe to the Child Support Agency. If you don't pay these, you can be taken to court and a judge can sanction the use of bailiffs to take your goods. Persistent failure to pay arrears can result in a prison sentence.

Income tax or VAT arrears

- HM Revenue & Customs (HMRC) stands first in line in the queue of creditors should you be forced to file for bankruptcy. It takes priority over all others. The tax authority is also the least likely to do a deal, often demanding a full repayment or a trip to court. You can be sent to prison for non-payment of income tax or VAT. Tax credit overpayments must also be repaid to HMRC, though these are often recouped from future payments.

Non-priority debts

These debts include:

Benefits overpayments

- Income Support, Jobseeker's Allowance and disability allowance all fall into this category.

Credit debts

- Credit debts, such as overdrafts, loans, hire purchase, credit card accounts and catalogues. They can send bailiffs to seize goods, but can be put off longer than priority debt.

Student loans

- Money borrowed from Student Loans Company to pay fees and maintenance.

Borrowed money

- Money borrowed from friends or family.

Water rates

- Your local water company will demand you pay annual water bills, but cannot cut you off if you refuse. You will need to pay the debt at some point, but it is classed as non-priority.

" Top of the list of arrears to be paid off should be mortgage or rent, fuel, council tax, court fines, maintenance payments and income tax and VAT. "

STEP 3: WORK OUT YOUR BUDGET

Now you have a good idea of how much you owe, you need to discover how much spare cash you have so that you can start planning how to keep the debt down each month. Use the following checklists, divided into income and expenses, to help you sort through your finances. An example showing how to lay out the information is given on pages 22–5.

To make your budget as useful as possible, write down your income and expenditure as monthly sums.

- If you receive any income weekly: multiply by 4.33 (if you multiply a weekly figure by four, you will end up leaving four weeks out of your annual total).
- For quarterly bills, divide by three.
- For shopping bills, it is probably easier to think of how much you spend per week and then multiply by 4.33.
- For holidays, consider your annual spend and divide by 12.
- For car and clothing expenditure, it might be helpful to look back through your statements and other records to ascertain an approximate yearly spend and, again, divide by 12.

Income

Under income, include:

- **Wages or salaries** for you and your partner, if you have one. Put in your net earnings, that is, after deductions. This should be the amount you regularly receive. If the amounts are different each month, average them over three or six months.
- **Guaranteed overtime.**
- **Any state benefits** you are paid: child benefit (including lone parent benefit), Jobseeker's Allowance, Income Support, Tax Credits, Child Tax Credit, incapacity benefit or other disability benefit.
- **Any pensions.**
- **Any income from savings.**
- **Maintenance** from an ex-partner for you or your children. Include any child support from the Child Support Agency (CSA).
- **Contributions** from other members of your family and any lodgers.

> **"** Once you know what you owe, start planning how to keep the debt down each month. **"**

 There are things you can do to help increase your income, such as claiming benefits if you are unemployed or taking on an extra job if you are employed. For more details, see pages 117-20. For information on potential benefits, see pages 120-3.

Expenses

Under expenses, include everything you currently spend money on over the year, but divide them into three categories:

Essential spending

- **Housing costs.** This should include your mortgage or rent. If you have taken out a second mortgage or **secured loan** against the property, include this bill. Also add buildings and contents insurance, service charges and ground rent.
- **Life or endowment insurance cover** attached to your mortgage.
- **Insurance** that is not part of your housing costs, such as mobile phone insurance.
- **Council tax.**
- **Utility charges.**
- **Telephone charges,** including mobile phone bills.
- **Childcare** costs.
- **TV licence** and any TV rental costs.
- **Any other essential expenses,** such as medical and dental expenses or support for an elderly relative.
- **Money you should set aside** for unexpected events and contingencies. This includes saving for things like the replacement of essential household goods when they break down.

Everyday spending

- **Housekeeping.** Look at your last food bill. Include realistic amounts for what you spend on food, toiletries, cleaning materials, sweets, children's pocket money and pet food.
- **Meals at work.**
- **Travel expenses.** Include both public transport and the cost of running a car, such as road tax, insurance and maintenance.
- **School expenses,** such as private school fees, travel to school, school dinners, uniform and extra curricular activies.
- **Laundry.**
- **Cigarettes** and alcohol.
- **Hobbies,** e.g. annual membership to a golf or tennis club, specialist sports equipment.

Occasional spending

- **Clothing**
- **Entertainment,** such as DVD rentals, CD purchases, trips to the cinema and theatre
- **Magazines/newspapers**
- **Birthdays**
- **Holidays**
- **House repairs**

Monthly budget plan

INCOME	AMOUNT (£s)
Wage/salary: you	
- your partner	
Guaranteed overtime: you	
- your partner	
Benefits: child benefit (including lone parent)	
- Jobseeker's Allowance	
- Income Support	
- Tax Credits	
- Child Tax Credit	
- incapacity benefit or other disability benefits	
Any pensions: you	
- your partner	
Any income from savings: you	
- your partner	
Maintenance	
Child support from the CSA	
Contributions from members of family/lodgers	
Any other form of income	

TOTAL INCOME

Essential spending

EXPENDITURE	AMOUNT (£s)
Mortgage/rent	
Secured loan/second mortgage	
Buildings insurance	
Contents insurance	
Service charges	
Ground rent	
Life/endowment insurance cover	
Other insurance: mobile phone	
– pet health	
– car	
Council tax	
Electricity	
Gas	
Oil/solid fuel	
Water rates	
Telephone: landline/broadband	
– mobile	
Childcare	
– child support costs	
Television licence	
Television rental	
Other essential expenses: medical	
– dental	
– other	
Contingencies	
Essential spending expenditure to carry over to page 25	

23

Monthly budget plan (continued)

Everyday spending

EXPENDITURE	AMOUNT (£s)
Food bills	
Toiletries	
Cleaning materials	
Sweets	
Children's pocket money	
Pet food	
Meals at work	
Travel expenses: public transport	
– vehicle fuel	
– road tax	
– maintenance	
School expenses: fees	
– travel to school	
– school dinners	
– uniform	
– private lessons	
– after school clubs (sports, music, etc.)	
Laundry	
Cigarettes	
Alcohol	
Hobbies	
– membership fee(s)	
– equipment	
Everyday spending expenditure to carry over to page 25	

Occasional spending

EXPENDITURE	AMOUNT (£s)
Clothing	
Entertainment: DVD rentals	
- CD purchases	
- trips to the cinema/theatre	
- other	
Magazines/newspapers	
Birthdays	
Holidays	
House repairs	
Occasional spending expenditure to carry over below	

Essential spending expenditure carried over from page 23	
Everyday spending expenditure carried over from page 24	
Occasional spending expenditure carried over from above	

TOTAL EXPENDITURE	

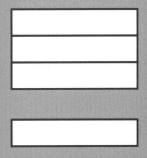

“Group your outgoing expenses according to whether they are essential, everyday or occasional. ”

STEP 4: DO YOUR SUMS

When you've added up all the figures and deducted your total expenditure from your total income, you will see if you have any money left over in order to pay your debts.

That makes it sound like a breeze, but leaving out vital costs such as council tax payments or an invitation to a relative's wedding (which you must attend and that means spending some money), is easily done and can knock your calculations. The worst thing to come out of your budgeting is if it allows you to carry on spending beyond your means. So:

- Look through your bank statements to check which organisations you pay by direct debt and how much.
- Check standing orders and any other regular payments.
- See how often you withdraw money from a cash machine and think about what you pay for in cash rather than with a debit card or credit card.
- Look at any credit card or store card bills to see if there are any regular payments made (you might be paying for insurance cover for payments on the card using that account). Also check how much you pay off each month – are you reducing the balance or just paying the interest?

- If you have any hire purchase contracts, check which account is making the monthly payments and how much for. The same goes for car loans or any other personal loans that you need to maintain.

Almost everyone who goes through this process finds that some savings can be made from somewhere. In its simplest form it may mean cutting back on things that you consider part of your basic lifestyle. That might be a regular trip to the pub or a low-cost airline city-break or a Saturday night takeaway and DVD habit. For the time being, until the debts are on the way down, put these luxuries on hold. The savings you will make can go towards your effort to cut the debt. Whatever you can do without, it will all help.

This information provides you with a valuable overview of how your finances are structured. It will also form the foundation for a budget and action plan that you will then need to draw up to help you out of your debt problem – this is explained on pages 136–8.

❝ Almost everyone finds that they can make savings somewhere. ❞

For more information on how credit cards work and how the providers make money out of them, see pages 50–62. If you have large credit card bills, turn to pages 63–6, which explain how to deal with that form of debt.

Case Study Zoe Finch

Office manager Zoe Finch, 37, found herself with £45,000 of debts on loans and credit cards after she embarked on a series of home improvements, including a new kitchen. She soon found her overdraft increasing as she struggled to maintain her debt repayments.

After a visit to a debt advice charity she drew up a chart showing her income and outgoings. The list of her outgoings revealed she had a costly magazine habit and was buying clothes that when she looked in her wardrobe she realised were never worn. Eating in restaurants had become a regular part of her social life, as had eating takeaways and ready meals. Spending on every comfort for her cat was also eating into her disposable income.

Ms Finch realised that she could lose her flat if she failed to rein in her spending and reorganise her debts. So she cut down on unnecessary spending and approached her bank about reducing her debt payments. It recommended she consolidate her credit card and loan debts in one super loan. Ms Finch rejected this advice in favour of switching the credit card balances to interest-free cards and re-mortgaging a year later to consolidate her debts. She cut up her other credit cards.

Lenders explained

There are many different organisations eager to lend us money – from high street banks and debt-consolidation companies to doorstep lenders. This section looks across the spectrum at the different types of lenders, how they operate and what it means for your debts.

WHO IS LENDING MONEY?

Lending money is sometimes likened to a confidence trick, a trick that means we only need keep a small amount of capital to one side to facilitate billions of pounds of credit. To put it rather crudely, banks take in savings and promise to pay an interest rate. They then lend that money to customers who promise to pay it back with interest. The interest on saving costs the banks much less than they charge customers who borrow money. How much of a difference there is determines how much profit the bank makes.

A bank will usually pay a saver a little below the Bank of England base rate and the borrower will be charged a little more than the bank's base rate for a mortgage and much higher if they want an unsecured loan. For example, if the Bank of England base rate is 5.5 per cent, which is the case at the time of writing, then most savings accounts will be 5 per cent or below. Most mortgage rates will be 6 per cent or above. Most unsecured rates will be 7 per cent or above and credit card and overdraft lending will be 13 per cent or above.

You will see bargain basement offers advertised on the television and in newspapers and bank branches for all types of savings and loans. Savings rates can be as high as 10 per cent and mortgage rates can be as low as 2 or 3 per cent, but they are almost always introductory offers that last a few months or a year at most. In the case of mortgages, low introductory rates usually come with a serious catch and that is staying with the same lender for several years after the introductory offer has finished and on a much higher interest rate (see annual equivalent rate on page 41 for more information).

Likewise cash-back mortgages look enticing, but the 'gift' of thousands of

 For information about interest rates, see the section 'Understanding interest rates' on pages 39–41.

pounds always comes with a catch – either a much higher interest rate than rival mortgages or a lock-in period tying you to the provider.

Banks make huge profits in part because they are allowed to lend much more than they take in savings. If the savers all wanted their money back, the banking industry knows there isn't enough cash in the system to do it and the banks would be forced to close, just as they do in the movies when there is a collapse in confidence and a 'run on the bank'. But they make a calculation, overseen by the financial watchdogs, that they have enough cash to cover most events.

Charles Dickens wrote about Britain's ordinary working people and often mentioned how he thought the banking system, then in its infancy, was a kind of conjuring trick. He came to the view that: 'Credit is a system whereby a person who cannot pay gets another person who cannot pay to guarantee that he can pay.'

In today's consumer society that means you go to a shop without any cash and ask to buy goods with credit. You hand over a card that says the bank or credit card company will pay, except it doesn't really have the money.

To Dickens, the bank is the guarantor knowing it doesn't really have the cash to cover the debt. It tells us it's alright to spend money that we haven't got and it hasn't got. Of course, today, banks are much more complicated beasts, but at heart the same conjuring trick applies, and as long as savers keep their money in the bank, customers can continue borrowing from the bank.

In the nineteenth century, building societies emerged to challenge the banks as lenders, though almost exclusively on home loans. In the last ten years, a myriad of firms have appeared with the sole aim of tempting you to borrow money. The only difference between them is that different rules are attached, resulting in different risks and different interest rates.

> **❝ If everyone wanted all their money back from the bank at the same time, there wouldn't be enough cash in the system to pay it all. ❞**

A call for greater transparency

A report made by the Social Justice Policy Group in 2006 for the Conservative party argued that personal debt was the biggest social problem facing the country and a major factor in family breakdown. The report said it believed 11 million families were facing relationship problems as a result of debt worries. It attacked high street banks and loan companies for not exercising 'due care' when lending money and called for 'complete transparency' in the selling of credit, so that people knew how much interest they would have to pay.

BANKS

We may complain about the banks, but they are still far and away the largest providers of credit in the UK. Their presence on every major high street has kept them ahead in the race to sell loans and credit cards and mortgages. However, they rarely offer the best deals, so when you are managing your debts, it is important to shop around to cut your monthly payments.

"Banks rarely offer the best deals, even though they are the largest credit providers. "

What accounts are available?

Through thick and thin you will need to maintain a bank account. There are current accounts, deposit accounts and accounts that are either stripped-down versions of current accounts – the basic bank account – or turbo-charged current accounts – the packaged accounts.

Many debt advisers recommend opening an internet current account if you have web access. These accounts allow you to monitor your income and outgoings on a daily basis. This gives you the chance to avoid late payment fees and other charges that result simply from you missing vital payment dates. Bank charges are a huge factor in the debts of many people. They can quickly mount up and turn a bad situation into a drama. Go for the internet accounts without bells and whistles – you just need an account that takes your salary and pays out direct debits and standing orders. You won't need the extra insurances and other offers that come with packaged accounts.

Current accounts The most familiar bank account. Gives you a chequebook and cheque card, a facility that allows you to withdraw cash at cash points up to a maximum level each day. You can pay bills and deposit cash and cheques at branches.

Basic bank accounts Basic bank accounts are available from most high street banks and cater for people who find it hard to get a standard current account, often because they have a poor credit record. A basic bank account is the same as a current account except that you won't get an overdraft facility, a chequebook or a cheque card. You will, however, get a cashcard that allows you to withdraw cash from an ATM. You will also be able to use the bank's branches for other transactions. If you do not have access

 For more information on basic bank accounts and what they can and cannot do for you, see pages 187–90.

to the internet or your finances are already in a parlous state (and internet banks have rejected you), you will need a basic bank account.

Packaged bank accounts These accounts offer a standard current account with some extra facilities. Sometimes you get your own personal adviser, sometimes it is just some products bundled together. Sometimes you get both. What you always get is a monthly bill for maintaining the accounts.

More than eight million people in the UK pay for packaged accounts, netting the banks at least £850 million each year. Most offer a small range of benefits, including free or discounted travel insurance and car breakdown cover. Which? research shows that many bank customers are persuaded to pay for their current account when it is, in reality, of little benefit. For example, HSBC Plus costs £155.40 a year and the only really useful benefit is travel insurance, which is not much use when you are deep in debt. (It also gives card protection and ID theft insurance, but

neither is worth having because these protection insurances are covered by the bank anyway, especially ID theft, which is the bank's responsibility and not yours.) Lloyds TSB customers who pay to maintain their accounts face even higher fees as Lloyds charges £300 a year.

Savings accounts The difference between savings rates and loan rates shows that it pays to cut down on credit before you begin saving. If you have a regular savings plan, you should consider suspending further contributions. Check the small print of your savings plan to see if there are penalties for stopping payments. Most don't have penalties and you should be fine. Some people make their deposit account the centre of their finances and accept the restrictions on withdrawals they usually impose. The strict regime keeps some people from going back to their free-spending ways, but an internet account is probably a better bet because of the flexibility it gives and the clear view of your finances on a day-to-day basis.

Money management tip

If you are in debt and serious about tackling the problem, you need to switch from a packaged bank account to a free current account. If your bank won't let you, then switch bank.

❝ Which? research shows that many bank customers who pay for their current account get little real benefit. **❞**

Banks get tougher

Banks have come under increased scrutiny by government regulators and been told their current penalty account charges are unfair. In response, some have tightened their lending criteria and restricted facilities, such as overdrafts. Interest rates on overdrafts have also crept upwards.

HSBC said recently that increasing numbers of customers saw their current

Overdrafts

An overdraft is designed as a temporary loan attached to your current account. The trouble is that recent studies show most of us use it on a regular basis. Most banks will give you an overdraft limit within which you must pay interest charges, but no extra fees. Beyond this limit you will need to pay an arrangement fee, which could be a one-off fee or need renewing on a regular basis.

If you exceed your overdraft limit, you will have an unauthorised overdraft and you will incur hefty charges. Even an authorised overdraft may carry charges, such as an arrangement fee and/or a usage fee that you pay each month or quarter that your account is overdrawn.

account overdraft as the most flexible of their debt facilities. Many younger bank customers, and especially first-time homebuyers, were rolling sizeable overdrafts from one month to the next without ever paying them off. Even though banks charge anywhere between 11 and 16 per cent interest on authorised overdrafts, they don't like the uncertainty of overdraft lending. HSBC subsidiary First Direct has imposed a £10-a-month fee on customers and other banks are expected to follow suit. For the time being, though, many accounts include a small free overdraft. Some give a larger interest-free limit of £100 or £250 – be careful, though, as

For information on how to challenge bank charges that you feel have been unfairly levied, see pages 197-203.

Overdraft checklist

If you always have an overdraft at the end of each month, you need to find out:

- How much you are going overdrawn.
- How much you are paying in interest.
- Are there any fees and charges for maintaining an overdraft?
- If there are charges you don't understand, contact your bank.

This is information you need before you can begin tackling overdraft bills. Once you have brought the costs down (or not) you need to include the payments in your monthly budget planner.

If your situation gets out of hand, you will also need this information available when you draw up a debt management plan.

they may have high overdraft interest rates once you go above these limits.

Overdraft rates are three to four percentage points lower than credit card interest rates, and that appears to be the main attraction to customers that use their credit limits to the full. But if you are going to get your debts under control, you need to get your overdraft under control as well.

Who are the big lenders?

Over the last 20 years, banks have done their best to ruin their reputations. From allegations of scandalously poor service to the most recent clampdown by the Office of Fair Trading on unfair bank penalty charges, the banks have milked their customers while giving little in return.

To get round their reputation problem, many of them sell products through different brands. Cheltenham & Gloucester is one of the largest mortgage lenders and gains many customers through mortgage brokers and TV advertising, but the bulk of its sales are first and foremost to customers of its owner, Lloyds TSB.

Barclays sells mortgages through its Woolwich brand and secured loans through its Firstplus offshoot. Firstplus, which is advertised by TV personality Carol Vorderman, has been the subject of several complaints to newspapers and consumer watchdogs for taking a heavy handed approach to recouping debts. Few of its customers will know that the company is owned by Barclays.

Halifax sells all its main banking products under its own brand. Royal Bank of Scotland owns NatWest. Abbey, another of the biggest mortgage lenders, is owned by Spanish bank Santander.

❝ Many banks sell their products through different brands. ❞

 See pages 136–8 for how to create and use a debt management plan to reduce your overdraft and other debts.

Cash machines

Whatever type of account you have, access to cash machines is free in almost all cases. The only cash machines you have to pay to use are convenience cash points, often found in garages, pubs and shops. Where these are run by banks and building societies, an on-screen message should warn if you're going to be charged. Other providers are not covered by the Banking Code, but they should nevertheless tell you whether you will be charged, in which case try not to use them.

> **"** Plenty of studies show that building societies offer better rates of interest, especially in their traditional mortgage business. **"**

BUILDING SOCIETIES

To its supporters, **mutuality** pays handsome **dividends**. The dividend isn't paid to **shareholders**, as in banks, but it is paid back to customers – the members. In the case of building societies, there have been plenty of studies to show that they offer better rates of interest, especially in their traditional mortgage business. The largest building society, Nationwide, often tops best-buy tables for its standard variable rate, which is consistently lower than bank standard variable rates. Independent data provider Moneyfacts said in a recent report that building societies generally sold more competitive products than banks (although – also according to Moneyfacts – banks offered a more diverse range of products).

A local building society can also be more accommodating than a bank branch, which generally has less flexibility to talk about the best way to solve your debt problems. However, that is not always the case. Mutuality is not always a byword for sympathy and generosity. Building societies have been found selling products to people in debt that are completely inappropriate, just as the big banks have.

Some building societies still allow customers to use a passbook to deposit and withdraw cash, which many people,

For more about mortgages and the benefits offered by building societies, see pages 88–105.

usually elderly people, like so they can see easily how much money they have in their account.

LOAN COMPANIES

Secured and unsecured loans are two of the most profitable products that finance companies can sell (see pages 68–80). For that reason, the number of companies selling loans seems endless. The banks are the biggest operators, mainly because they are well placed to persuade customers to convert overdrafts into loans. The classified advertising sections of local newspapers and tabloid national newspapers are also full of adverts for loans.

Many of the companies specialise in **consolidation loans**, which allow people with several loans to put them together in one loan, often with a top-up to release some extra cash. Firstplus, Norton Finance, Loans.co.uk and Ocean Finance are four of the biggest operators and, as with the products from all the other consolidation loan firms, most debt advisers will tell you their products are a bad deal. If your debts are in such a bad way that you consider a consolidation loan, it would be better to sort out the problems than borrow more money.

Loan companies either charge fees, which are added to the loan; sell a

---

Jargon buster

Consolidated loans If you have multiple debts with different lenders – on credit cards, loans, with friends and family – you can shift them all to a single loan, also known as a debt consolidation loan. You can consolidate debts in a personal loan or an unsecured loan

Dividends An annual payment made by companies out of their profits to their shareholders. It repays the investment made by shareholders in the company. Building societies and other mutual organisations don't have shareholders. They re-invest their profits into making their mortgages and other products cheaper for their members (their customers become members when they buy a product from a building society)

Life insurance If you die, this insurance cover will pay a lump sum to your partner or whoever inherits your estate. If you are the main wage earner and don't have life insurance, your partner could be left to pay a mortgage and other bills on a low income. Always check if life insurance is paid via your pension, if you have one of course

Mutuality Some businesses are owned by their members and these mutual organisations give their profits back to members in the form of cheaper products

Shareholders People who own a share in a limited company; can also be institutions such as pension funds

secured loan that puts your house at risk; or sell a loan so big the payments quickly become unaffordable. Consumers also complain at extortionate charges for redeeming consolidation loans early.

Even if the four firms mentioned are innocent of the above charges, debt advisers still recommend against consolidation loans because the costs of the loans are high, as are the risks of losing your home when the loan is secured against a property.

CREDIT UNIONS

Credit unions are financial co-operatives owned and controlled by their members (see the box, below). They offer loans as well as savings that lack the kind of small

---

More about credit unions

The government has put a good deal of time into promoting credit unions. It sees them as a safe haven for people who find it difficult getting a bank account and a loan from mainstream lenders.

Each credit union has a 'common bond', which determines who can join it. The common bond may be for people living or working in the same area, people working for the same employer or people who belong to the same association, such as a church or trade union. Most credit unions loans will cost you no more than 1 per cent a month on the reducing balance of the loan (an APR of 12.7 per cent), though legally they can charge double that. Make sure you check the rate you will pay.

Importantly, credit union loans come with no hidden charges and no penalties for repaying the loan early. When so many people are sticking with expensive overdrafts because they like the flexibility, a flexible loan such as this should be attractive.

Life insurance is built in, at no cost to the borrower, so if you were to die before you had repaid the loan, insurance would repay the lot for you.

The credit union association Abcul (www.abcul.org) says that when you borrow from a credit union, you may carry on saving, meaning that by the time you finish repaying the loan, your savings will have continued to grow.

Most credit unions can lend for up to five years (unsecured) and up to ten years (secured). Some credit unions can lend for up to ten years (unsecured) and up to 25 years (secured).

 For further information on loan consolidation companies, see page 73. To find your nearest credit union, go to www.abcul.org or look in your local Yellow Pages/ Thomson directory.

print and penalties imposed by banks and building societies. After a few went bust in the early part of the decade, the government introduced strict regulation to protect members' cash. Not all areas have a credit union, but they are a growing sector and new ones are opening all the time.

CATALOGUES

Littlewoods, Next Directory and La Redoute have recently been joined by Tesco in the catalogue business. If you buy clothes, furniture or any other goods from them, they will often give you credit, allowing you to buy now and pay later. Any debts you have with a catalogue company will need to be added to your list of outstanding payments that need to be covered. Typically, catalogue companies will charge rates of interest akin to store cards – between 20 and 25 per cent per year.

> **❝Hire purchase agreements have come back into fashion as consumers seek to discipline their repayments. ❞**

RETAILERS

Hire purchase agreements are another form of debt along with interest-free deals for the purchase of everything from cookers to sofas. Typically, a hire purchase agreement is a contract between you and the store to pay back the sum owed over a set period of time. They have come back into fashion as consumers seek to impose more discipline on their repayments. Interest-free deals also get the hard sell. Some furniture stores, for example, will allow you to take delivery of a sofa and not pay for four years. It may seem like a good deal because it is interest free, but it is still an overhanging debt that you are committed to repay.

HOME CREDIT FIRMS

The £1.3 billion-a-year doorstep lending market appears to be uncompetitive and, as a result, customers may be paying too much for their loans. This was the verdict of the government's Competition Commission in 2006. Provident Financial, Cattles, S&U and London Scottish Bank are among the institutions that use local agents to offer loans to people in their homes at interest rates that can be as high as 900 per cent APR. They tend to target poorer communities, which often do not have easy access to other forms of credit.

For more information about hire purchase agreements, see pages 76–8. They are discussed under the heading 'Loan-type agreements'.

The National Consumer Council said in a complaint about the industry that many low-income families have little choice but to use this form of credit because their credit score with mainstream lenders would be low. A typical loan of £100 for six months involves the borrower paying back £160.

" Many low-income families have little choice but to use home credit firms because of their low credit score. "

LOAN SHARKS

Loan sharking is often carried out by criminal gangs who target vulnerable members of the community and is a completely unregulated area of finance. During 2006 and 2007, the government ran a series of pilot projects aimed at prosecuting loan sharks. A report for the government found that many self-employed people relied on loan sharks for work, borrowing money to buy tools and equipment. Extortionate rates of interest were charged – in one case a £150 loan had a 1,000 per cent interest rate over six months, giving a repayment of £285. Violence was threatened if the businesses failed to keep up repayments.

Home credit firms are licensed to offer credit under the Consumer Credit Act, though they are not allowed to canvas for business or cold call anyone. They must follow leads based on recommendations. By contrast, loan sharks illegally sell without a licence.

Understanding interest rates

More people understand fractions than they do percentages.
Unfortunately the cost of borrowing money is almost always expressed
in terms of percentage interest rates.

To confuse us further, banks over the years have developed several different measures of interest rates with the result that percentage interest rates are not calculated the same way from one bank to another.

You don't need to be too cynical to think it is a deliberate attempt to bamboozle the public. Which? thinks the system is confusing. It sent an official complaint to the government's consumer watchdog the Office of Fair Trading. A report from the OFT is not expected until 2008. While the OFT decides what to say about interest rates, you need to get to grips with them now.

To illustrate the effect of interest rates on a loan, here are some examples of different charges.

AN INTRODUCTORY RATE

A mortgage these days almost always comes with two separate interest rates – an introductory rate and a **standard variable rate** (SVR), which applies when

Jargon buster

Annual equivalent rate (AER) This figure appears as a percentage and illustrates the total cost/benefit over a year. In other words, what the interest rate would be if the interest was added to your account once each year. It is usually applied to savings and excludes any bonus interest that may be payable

Annual percentage rate (APR) The APR is the rate of interest that you agree to pay on money that you borrow. It is an average over the term of the loan/mortgage including any discounts and fees

Standard variable rate (SVR) The rate charged for mortgages that are NOT on a special deal. Introductory mortgage offers revert to the SVR when they come to the end of the offer period

Working out the percentage rate

A percentage is the same as saying one per hundred. If you see an advert for a loan saying 1% (or 1 per cent), it is telling you that for every £100 you borrow, you will pay £1 in interest. If the interest rate is 12 per cent over a year – and most loan rates are expressed as an **annual percentage rate** (APR) – then for every £100 you borrow, you will pay £12 a year. If you borrow £5,000 at 12 per cent, you will pay £600 a year in interest. The more you borrow, therefore, the more interest you pay.

the introductory rate has run its course. The introductory rate could be 5.39 per cent with a 6.79 per cent SVR. People who switch their mortgages when the introductory offer runs out usually pay attention to the first figure and not the second. There is intense competition among lenders to attract new customers and low introductory offers are the chief way they turn heads and get people interested.

People who want to take out a mortgage and stick with that lender for a long time will pay more attention to the SVR figure and how it compares with rival lenders. That's because the SVR will apply to the mortgage for the remainder of its term once the introductory offer has run out. All mortgage lenders have an SVR and you should ask to see it if it doesn't appear on any literature.

On adverts for a mortgage you won't see a figure for the SVR. Instead, lenders must give the annual percentage rate (APR) alongside their introductory offer. An APR includes all costs associated with the loan, such as interest, fees and any compulsory insurances. It also includes the introductory rate and is therefore an average of the introductory offer and the SVR. It was designed to allow consumers to compare products on a like-for-like basis: every lender must quote this rate by law.

ANNUAL PERCENTAGE RATE (APR)

Personal loans also use the APR to show how much a loan will cost. Interest is charged on the whole loan and the payments spread out over an agreed period, usually three or five years. You can ask the lender to send you a schedule of payments. They will also supply leaflets illustrating how much you would pay each month for borrowing different sums. Usually, the larger the sum borrowed, the lower the interest rate. To illustrate how paying loans at different rates affects the cost, see the chart, left.

Loan repayments

This chart shows how much interest would be paid on a loan of £1,000 and £10,000 over varying periods and varying APRs.

£1,000	Lender 1	Lender 2
	6% loan	16% loan
3 years	£93	£247
5 years	£156	£426

£10,000	Lender 1	Lender 2
	6%	16%
3 years	£926	£2,468
5 years	£1,555	£4,253

 For more information on mortgages and understanding the different interest rates that are applied, see pages 88–105.

Credit cards use the APRs but calculate interest on monthly balances. If you only pay the minimum contribution each month, you can find that interest charges mean you never pay the bill. For instance, if you have a balance of £10,000 at 16 per cent APR, you could spend 50 years making payments and never get rid of the bill. In the meantime, you will have spent £19,631 on interest payments.

OVERDRAFT RATE

Bank overdraft rates of interest vary widely. Some will charge as low as 11.9 per cent, others as much as 18.9 per cent. The common factor is that they tend to have one rate for authorised overdrafts and another for unauthorised. The unauthorised interest rate is usually much higher – more like 25 per cent or so.

Like a credit card interest rate, an overdraft rate is applied to a variable loan that can go up and down depending on how much you pay off the debt. Usually, overdrafts get out of control when you are fined penalty charges and they are added to the debt and interest is applied to the whole sum.

ANNUAL EQUIVALENT RATE (AER)

The interest rates on savings products are shown as an AER when calculated monthly or quarterly. It is supposed to demonstrate the effect of compound interest. In a way, we talk about compound interest in relation to credit cards. It means the previous month's gain is added to the next month and the interest calculated on the total. In this way, your growing investment attracts higher interest payments as time goes on and the interest payments keep being added to the overall total. It normally excludes bonus interest.

❝ If you only pay off the mininum amount on your credit card, you could make payments for 50 years and never get rid of the original bill. ❞

For more information on personal loans, see pages 69–70.
For more information on bank overdrafts, see pages 32–3.

Your credit report

How well you are treated by banks, mortgage lenders and loan companies depends, to a large extent, on your credit rating. It is hard to escape the information held by the credit reference agencies showing how you manage your finances. They can almost seem like an extension of Big Brother – always watching and noting the big financial decisions you take.

Every time you apply for credit, lenders will usually run a check on you with a credit reference agency. The agencies compile detailed financial files on almost every adult, and lenders use this and other information to decide whether or not they should give you credit. If they agree to a loan, the information also helps them decide what interest rate they will charge.

It's not the only information they use. Mortgage companies, in particular, will often ask many more questions about your current circumstances, your income and outgoings, to compile a picture of your lifestyle. But in the end, it is your credit history that is the key to opening doors to cheaper credit and credit with fewer strings attached.

❝ Your credit history is the key to cheaper credit with fewer strings, and, contrary to myth, family and friends are not included on your individual credit file. ❞

CREDIT RATING MYTHS

Before setting out how credit reports are compiled, it is interesting to ask what a credit report is not. There are many myths about credit reports, which can distort how you go about tackling your debts.

The most recent piece of research on the subject found that around half of all adults did not fully understand what a credit report is, with a significant number misled by 'credit folklore'. Almost two-thirds believed the activities of family and friends can harm their credit report. Another large section believed the credit reference agencies make the decision on whether you should get a loan or credit card and that there is a 'hit list' of people who should be refused credit.

In fact, family and friends are not included on a credit file unless they share a bank account, credit card or mortgage with you. It is also the lenders and not the agencies who make the decision about who should receive an offer of a loan, based on their own criteria and not a 'hit list' of people or properties.

To counter accusations of Big Brotherdom, the credit reference agencies

Jargon buster

Credit score Your credit history is held
on several credit reference agency
databases and credit card companies
and banks look at your credit history
and give you a score. Each company
uses its own scoring method

also point out that lenders' credit scores
exclude your sex, race, religion, political
beliefs, sexuality and criminal record.
Employment and medical records are
also excluded.

WHAT'S IN YOUR CREDIT REPORT?

There are three main credit reference
agencies – Experian, Callcredit and
Equifax. They store records on vast
databases using information about your
finances from pretty much all your
lenders, and the records also include
details of the electoral roll, county court
judgements, bankruptcies and past and
present credit commitments.

Application details

These are the details you supplied when
you asked for your report. They are used
to produce the report.

Electoral roll information

This is the starting point for establishing
who you are. An agency will also know
how long you have lived at your current
address and previous addresses in the
last seven years. If anybody else has
used your address to access credit or if

there are any other discrepancies
between the name you have given and
that on your file, then you can be turned
down. At the least it makes searching for
your details difficult, at the worst it
makes the lenders think you've
deliberately sought to mislead them.

Aliases

Aliases are created when lenders tell the
credit agency of other names you have
been known by or when you tell them of
other names you have used. Your credit
report will include information recorded in
these other names at the addresses you
provided when you applied for your
report.

Financial associations

Financial associations are details of
anyone you are financially connected to.
Financial connections are created by joint
accounts, joint applications, joint court
judgements or from information you have
given to the credit agency. When you
apply for credit, a lender may take into
account financial information about
people you are financially connected to.

County court judgements and bankruptcy information

Court judgements and individual
voluntary arrangements or bankruptcy
information are documented on your file
and if you've suffered any, you can
expect to find it much harder to get
credit. If someone else has used your
address to commit a fraud, then it can
taint your file, too. All records are

43

automatically removed from your report after six years except in the case of bankruptcy restriction orders that last more than six years. They will remain on file as long as they last.

Credit account information

Credit account information shows details of your credit agreements with lenders. If you have any queries about this credit account information and would like to contact the lender yourself, there is a list of useful addresses at the end of your report.

Settled accounts are kept on file for six years from the settlement date. The status history in respect of a settled account relates to the period of time prior to the date of settlement. Similarly, a defaulted account is removed from your report after six years, whether or not you have paid the debt in full. If you have paid off some of the debt, the balance should show how much you still owe.

Council of Mortgage Lenders (CML) information

Members of the CML record information on customers who have given up their homes or had them repossessed. If you have any queries about the CML information shown and would like to contact the company concerned yourself, there is a list of useful address at the end of your report. CML information may be recorded at up to three addresses – an address that was repossessed or surrendered and your previous and forwarding address(es).

Previous searches

Previous searches show the names of organisations that have seen some or all of the information recorded on your credit report within the past 12 months. Searches of your credit report should all have been made with your consent. Most will relate to credit applications you have made but some may be routine checks by your lenders on accounts you already have. Unrecorded enquiries, quotations, identity verification checks and credit report applications are shown for you on your copy of your report but are not seen by lenders.

Financial associate searches

Financial associate searches show when your credit report information has been seen because someone you are financially connected to has made an application for credit. This information is recorded for you on your copy of your credit report only. It is not seen by lenders.

Linked addresses

Linked addresses are created by lenders when you move or when you tell the agency your previous addresses. This information shows addresses that you have been connected with.

CIFAS – The UK's Fraud Prevention Service

CIFAS information is displayed by address and so the information may not be in your name. This information helps protect innocent people from becoming victims of fraud. The rules of CIFAS mean that

> ❗ Until a few years ago, the activities of previous tenants or owners of your home could affect your credit score, but this is no longer the case. However, they can still appear on your file along with debts that were, in fact, incurred by fraudsters. You need to contact the credit reference agency to clear these notices from your file (see Useful addresses, pages 208-11).

you will never automatically be declined credit because there is CIFAS information on your report. If you feel that a CIFAS entry is incorrect in any way, you can either contact the member directly using that address or let the agency know exactly what you feel is wrong and why and they will contact the member of your behalf.

Gone Away Information Network (GAIN)

GAIN shows that an individual owes money and has moved without giving the lender a forwarding address. If you have any queries about this information, contact the company that gave the agency the information.

WHAT MAKES A GOOD CREDIT HISTORY?

Starting from a point where you are free of credit can be a disadvantage if you

suddenly need some. There are plenty of examples of people applying for a loan and being turned down because their credit file is effectively empty. Why? Because lenders want you to have a credit history. They just don't want you to have a bad history. If they don't think they can make money from you, they are less keen to lend.

That means many lenders will reward you if you keep a rolling overdraft facility and maintain debt on your credit cards. This is not a sensible way to operate, but you can see what they mean. They think you are more likely to be someone who will pay their exorbitant rates of interest than someone who has obviously avoided high credit bills.

Likewise, if you make several applications for credit in a short space of time, you might harm your rating with lenders. Each time you apply for a loan or credit card, it appears on your file. You can look like you are shopping around and because the information is not shared by lenders, look like you are being rejected each time. Alternatively, you might appear a little bit desperate, another feature that many lenders dislike.

Your rights

If a shop or lender turns you down for credit, they should give you a clear explanation of the reason why. It is your right to know if their decision resulted from information on your credit file or their own policies on providing credit. It might be your income or the nature of your work that has a negative effect as much as your previous credit history.

Fictitious example of a credit report

Our reference: 00000000/A1
(Please quote on all correspondence)

Consumer Help Service
PO Box 9000
Nottingham NG80 7WP

Date of report: 1 February 2007

RR00000
MRS JESSICA SOMEBODY
186, HIGH STREET
ANYTOWN
MIDSHIRE
A12 4CD

DEAR MRS SOMEBODY

Your Credit Report
Thank you for your recent application for a credit report. This
includes all the information that we hold about you at the addresses
shown on page 2 of your report.

If you need to get in touch about the information on your report,
please remember to quote the reference number at the top of this
page. Please also provide the number of each item you are querying
(these are printed directly above the item they relate to, e.g. E1, C4,
P2). Information may be printed on both sides of the paper.

We have included a leaflet explaining the different types of information that may be included in your report and the steps you should take if you have any questions. Please use this leaflet to answer your queries. Most of the information we hold about you has been sent to us by companies with which you have a financial relationship or have had in the past.

Your credit report has been updated to include any other names you have been known by and with links to previous addresses. If any of this information is wrong and you believe it should be changed please contact us. The enclosed leaflet explains how to do this. Our records will also show that you made a request for your credit report. This information will not be seen by companies searching your credit report but will be shown on any reports you ask for in the future.

If you have any questions about the information companies have given to us, you may wish to get in touch with them because we need their authorisation to make changes to your report. A list of useful addresses is included at the back of your report.

Consumer Help Service

PS The quickest way to get help with your report is to call our helpdesk on 0870 241 6212 or log on to our website www.experian.co.uk. Click on Consumer Advice and visit Your Credit Report Help Centre.

The report then continues with separate sheets listing any of the information that relates to you described on pages 43-5. Explanatory leaflets are provided with the report.

How do I know my score?

You don't. The credit reference agencies store information in a particular format (see the example of a credit report, pages 46-7), but don't make the decisions or the score. Lenders access your reports and feed that information into their own systems. They have their own criteria for lending, which are always changing. Second-guessing which banks and loan companies are most likely to make a positive lending decision with the cheapest rate is a growing industry with websites such as www.moneyexpert.com, www.moneysaving expert.com and www.fool.co.uk constantly analysing the banks' moves.

ACCESSING YOUR CREDIT FILE

You can access information on your credit file either over the internet or by telephone or written request. Experian is the largest and most commonly used agency (see box, below). It offers customers a 30-day free trial of its service or a statutory credit check for £2. Callcredit and Equifax also charge £2, though Equifax encourages customers to buy a more comprehensive credit rating report for almost £15, which, it claims, is the nearest you will get to understanding why loan companies have rejected your request for credit. However, you should find all the information you need in the £2 version.

There are other companies, many of them operating on the internet, that claim for a fee that they can 'repair' your creditworthiness. The Office of Fair Trading recommends you steer clear of these firms because if there is anything wrong on your file, you can force the credit reference agency to change it for free. If you want to add an explanation of an event on your file, for instance a disputed debt or complaint about a lender, the agencies will help you. Or if it is debt advice you are after, there are several counselling services that offer bona fide free services (see pages 139–42).

There is, however, a positive way to influence your credit report, and that is to stabilise your debts and begin to pay them off.

> ❝ If there is anything wrong on your file, you can change it for free. ❞

Websites for the three main credit reference agencies are: www.experian.co.uk, www.callcredit.co.uk and www.equifax.co.uk.

Credit and store cards

If you have a balance on a credit card or store card, you could be wasting hundreds of pounds a year on interest and charges. A close look at those credit card bills could save you precious pounds that will cut your debt and is crucial in dealing with your debt problem. The first step towards getting debt under control is to ensure your credit cards, loans (pages 68-86) and mortgage (pages 87-105) are working efficiently.

2

Owning a credit card

As a nation we have more credit cards per head than any other bar the United States. We like to buy our clothes and furniture with credit cards and increasingly we need them to buy music, books and second-hand cars on the internet.

In 2006, the value of web purchases doubled from the previous year. By the end of 2007, experts predict another bumper year of spending on the net, much of it spent using credit cards.

The convenience of paying for something quickly and with a brief period of free credit – usually between 30 and 60 days – has helped encourage a decade-long consumer boom fuelled by debt. Yet a stigma remains around credit cards. A credit card debt is much worse in the minds of many people than an unsecured loan or a mortgage. The stigma is a result of our spending habits and prejudice. We take out a mortgage to buy a house, which is good. We apply for a loan to buy something specific, often a car – also good. On the other hand, a credit card is seen as something for profligate spenders with little or no control over their desire to frequent high street shops.

" High street stores have come to depend on their store cards to keep customers spending. "

USE BUT DON'T ABUSE

These days there are many reasons why someone might have credit card debts and making judgements about how it happened is not only hurtful but often misplaced. Studies have shown that only a small minority of people run up debts on credit cards without thinking how to pay it back. Financial illiteracy means they have probably misunderstood how interest rates work (see opposite) and how credit card charges can soon accumulate.

Then there are the banks and credit card companies that allow customers to run up debts without asking how they plan to pay it back. They are often accused of being irresponsible, yet they continue to lend without asking too many questions.

Store cards have also proved popular. A combination of easy credit at the point of sale and discounts of 10 per cent or more have proved irresistible to many shoppers. High street stores have come to depend on store cards to keep customers spending. For many people it is a convenient way to shop, but research has shown that around 20 per cent of cardholders keep a balance and have suffered interest rates in excess of 30 per cent.

Case Study | Emma Tomkinson

Emma Tomkinson, 33, lived on her own and spent beyond her means. She says that when she asked her bank for more credit to pay her debts it agreed. Within a few years she had two personal loans of £10,000 each and credit card debt of £6,000 – all with same lender. Ms Tomkinson was refused further credit on her existing card but allowed to add two more credit cards, each with a balance of £5,000. Another lender sanctioned three further credit cards. These were spent up to their maximum £5,000 limits. Next came a supermarket credit card that allowed her to spend more than £5,000.

In total, her loan debts amounted to £20,000 and her credit card debts totalled almost £40,000. Her initial spending spree had sent her over the limit. From that point onwards she had mainly borrowed to pay old debts and escalating penalty fees. She was on the point of mental exhaustion when she approached a debt adviser for help.

HOW CREDIT CARDS WORK

Maintaining credit card debt can be like all other forms of debt – it can be a savvy thing to do, but it can also be a route to trouble. Understanding how they work, including charges and rates – and how to avoid paying them – is essential to good credit card management.

Interest rate charges

Credit card interest charges apply to the balance you hold each month. All credit card companies calculate the charge in a slightly different way.

- **They give a set number of days free of interest:** some give 40 days, others almost 60 days. If you don't clear the previous month's balance, some credit card companies won't give you an interest-free period on new purchases.
- **Some then calculate the interest** on the balance of the sum detailed on your statement each month. From the moment you receive your statement you will have a set number of days to pay before you incur interest and late payments. This period will be the remainder of the interest-free period.
- **Others apply interest to the borrowed sum** in your account only a matter of days after they send a statement. These credit card companies (we can't name and shame them because they change all the time) often keep the date at which interest occurs in the small print. The date on the statement is the point at which you start incurring late payment penalty charges that kick in when you fail to pay the minimum payment specified.

❝ Some credit card companies calculate the interest on the monthly balance. ❞

Understanding your credit card statement

Available credit: The difference between the amount you have spent on the card and the credit limit, which is how much you have left to spend on the card. Be aware, the total balance on your card may be larger than that shown on your statement if you have made purchases using the card since the statement was issued

Balance transfer: The borrowings transferred from one card to another. Card companies want you to ditch your old card and move your debt to them. They will often provide an interest-free term up to a year or 18 months to encourage you to switch your debt to their card, but will charge up to 3 per cent of the balance as a fee. Often '0 per cent' transfers are advertised with a time limit, maybe six months or a year before reverting to the standard rate or purchase rate

Cash annual rate: Always higher than the balance transfer or purchase rates, it is usually a punishing interest rate that applies to cash withdrawals using the card or cheques supplied by the card company. Some even treat the purchase of gift vouchers as a cash withdrawal

Cash limit: The amount the card company will allow you to withdraw in cash using the card

Credit limit: The amount of money you can spend on the card. Put another way, it is the total amount you can borrow. The limit is set by the card company and will mainly depend on your credit score, income and employment

Minimum payment: The amount you must pay each month to avoid a penalty charge of (maximum) £12. It is usually around 2 per cent of the balance, so a £5,000 balance will have a minimum payment of £100

Monthly repayment: The amount you decide to pay to reduce your balance. It can be sent to the card company as a cheque, paid in at a bank branch or by direct debit

Purchase annual rate: Like the balance transfer rate, it can be offered at '0 per cent' before reverting to a higher rate once the offer period has expired

Store cards

A store card offers credit up to an agreed limit to spend in a particular shop or chain of shops. Like credit cards, they offer an interest-free period after which interest is charged. Most department stores, clothes shops and high street stores will offer customers the opportunity to buy the things they want with a store card. They entice customers with a discount from the retail price. Some will include loyalty programmes, such as exclusive shopping nights and discounts on other services like travel insurance.

The cards have proved to be highly profitable for the stores because millions of people build up a balance on the card rather than pay off the debt at the end of their interest-free period each month.

The shops used to charge interest at upwards of 30 per cent per year, which gave rise to huge monthly bills for those people who failed to pay off the balance over several months. A review of store cards in 2006, however, brought a clampdown on sky-high interest rates. The Office of Fair Trading said an interest rate of 25 per cent was the limit that store card providers could charge. It also demanded more information on the terms and conditions of the cards at the point of sale. The crackdown and the resulting bad publicity has encouraged many people to pay off their balances and cut up their store cards.

Of course, if you can be disciplined about your spending and you clear balances each month, then the offers available on store cards can be worthwhile. But if you are reading this book because you are concerned about how to manage your debts, then it is best to cut out store cards, forget about the supposed benefits and if you need to buy things on a card, for instance on the internet or a holiday flight, use a credit card from a reputable lender in the best buy tables published by Which? or in newspapers and on newspaper websites (see page 100).

CREDIT CARD PITFALLS

Only half of credit cardholders pay off their balances at the end of each month. At the end of 2005, credit card debt alone came to £58 billion. By the end of 2006, a reduction in outstanding credit card balances had brought this figure down to £55 billion. The reduction was almost entirely among those people who could use savings to reduce their debts or those who could afford to consolidate their debts in their mortgage. Many of the people who maintain large balances are, by definition, those who cannot afford to cut their borrowings. They are also the group who can least afford to pay the extra charges recently imposed by the industry. Standard interest rates have increased during 2006 and 2007 by between 1 and 2 per cent. Some of Britain's biggest card companies have also introduced even higher rates for customers with poor credit scores (see pages 42–5).

‟Many people who maintain large balances on their credit cards cannot afford to pay the extra charges recently imposed by the industry.”

Balance transfer fees

In addition, the card companies have introduced charges on **balance transfers** of between 2 and 3 per cent. Balance transfer is the term applied to your borrowings that you transfer from one card to another. Card companies after your business will entice you with an interest-free term of up to a year or 18 months to encourage you to switch your debt to their card, but will charge up to 3 per cent of the balance as a fee.

Money management tip

With a 3 per cent charge, the up-front cost of a £5,000 debt transfer is £150. If you have to pay, choose the card with the longest introductory offer as that will spread the costs of the fee over the longest period. Usually, the better the balance transfer interest rate, the higher the balance transfer fee.

❝ Many people have been switched to the standard interest rate without their knowledge. ❞

Introductory offers

Stricter rules applied by the card companies on introductory offers means that thousands of people have found themselves switched, usually without their knowledge, to the standard interest rate. It happens when you break a rule in the small print. For instance, if you miss a payment by a few days and incur a late payment fee, you will be kicked off the introductory offer. Even if you successfully appeal against the late payment fee (see opposite) you also need to check you are still enjoying the introductory offer because the computer might still have removed you to the standard rate.

Monthly repayments

Higher monthly repayments are becoming standard. More credit card companies are insisting on at least 2 per cent of the debt being paid off each

Case Study Stephen Hargreaves

Stephen Hargreaves, 39, of Bristol had balances totalling £19,500 on interest-free credit cards. Two of the interest-free deals ran for six months, the other two for one year. When he came to switch one of his balances to rival card company interest-free deals, he discovered the card companies charged a fee worth 2 per cent of the balance, capped at £50, for processing the transfer. He accepted. When he came to switch the next balance, the deal was 2 per cent and no

cap. For each balance transfer he would need to pay at least £100 in charges. He decided to re-mortgage and consolidate £14,500 in his mortgage.

He kept the cost the same by extending the life of the mortgage by five years. The other £5,000 was put on an interest-free card for a year with a 3 per cent charge.

During the year, he reviewed his outgoings and began to reduce the debt by £150 a month.

month, which is £100 a month for someone with a £5,000 debt. If you can afford it, reducing the balance on your credit card is sensible because, even if you are not paying off the whole amount, reducing the balance cuts interest charges.

Late payment charges

Late payment charges can also be unfairly large. A recent review of bank and other credit card operator practices by the Office of Fair Trading (OFT) found that they were imposing unfair late payment charges on customers – sometimes £25 or £30. Experts said the credit card operators had introduced these hefty charges as a way to make up for losses on interest-free introductory offers. The OFT took action against the industry and restricted the card companies to imposing a fee of £12. The watchdog's decision was widely welcomed by Which? and other consumer groups, which said people who had paid excessive fees should appeal for them to be refunded.

Figures from the Association of Payment Clearing Services show that one in five cardholders were hit with default charges last year. But according to more recent reports, the ruling has spurred the credit card companies to find other ways

of charging. Further investigations have found them adding charges elsewhere (such as balance transfer charges and higher interest rates on cash withdrawals) and making even more profit than they were before.

Other hidden costs

While borrowing can help give respite if it is part of an overall rescue plan (see pages 136–8), increasing credit card debts is never the answer. Even if you decide that a transfer fee is worth paying or you find a card without a fee (see pages 60–2), there are still ways credit card companies seek to make money from you.

One of the best examples happens when you need to use a card during an offer period. If you buy something during this period with the card, you will be refused the special rate. Instead the new debt will immediately qualify for the card provider's standard rate.

Most card providers have also introduced rules that allow them to terminate introductory offer deals. The rules are in the small print of your contract and will give the company the power to revert customers to the standard rate if they break a rule. The most common reason given by card companies is when customers miss a monthly payment.

 For information on appealing for a refund, see pages 197–203, which also includes sample letters to help you on your way.

What are pre-pay cards and are they a better option than credit cards?

Pre-pay cards are a recent phenomenum. They allow you to put cash on the card and then spend it. They work on the Visa and Mastercard networks and so are accepted in most shops. To some people they are a convenient way to escape the shackles of their bank and other finance companies they might owe money to.

With pre-pay cards it is possible to take cash from your wage and charge up the card in one straightforward transaction. There is a belief among many users that if they are self-employed, their income and spending habits will therefore be kept away from the prying eyes of the tax authorities. However, there is a catch. While there is no interest rate – because customers cannot spend more than they have on the cards and therefore incur debts – there are charges to be aware of. The charging structures vary from card to card, but there is usually a signing on fee and a monthly management fee.

For someone with debts elsewhere, getting one of these cards is just an expensive attempt to run away. A day of reckoning awaits, which could be made much worse if other debts have been ignored.

CREDIT CARD NO-NOS

Even savvy credit card users can be caught out by some of the card company's sharpest practices. Make every effort to avoid the following traps.

Don't take out payment protection insurance

Payment protection insurance (PPI) is another money-spinner for the banks and card companies. This is a product designed to pay the balance on your card if you become ill or unemployed. Virtually identical products are sold by finance companies to cover payments on loans and mortgages and the most common type of policy works like this:

- You ask for a credit card from a credit card company.
- They ask you to buy insurance to cover monthly payments should you become ill or unemployed. The company quotes the cost of the insurance per day or per £100 of cover to make it look like a bargain.
- You agree.

Why is it such a bad deal? The answer is that the card company charges an extortionate rate for the insurance and then puts so many clauses into the small print that it is virtually impossible to make a claim.

For example, one credit card charges 79p for every £100 of your monthly balance. That is equal to £39.50 each month on a £5,000 balance. After one year, you will have spent £474 on the insurance, which is added to your bill automatically. Yet it covers only 10 per cent of the total amount outstanding on your balance when you claim. Interest is still racking up and you will still be left with a sizeable bill. Other policies can be worse. They will only pay the minimum payment and your balance will grow while you are ill or unemployed. (See the table, below, for comparisons of the potential cost of taking out a PPI.)

Which? has described PPI cover as a rip-off and a form of profiteering by the industry. Which? research has shown that it is a bad deal for almost everyone and the research has also highlighted

Money management tips

- You can cancel the deal any time. So, if you are currently paying for one of these policies (and millions of people are without knowing it), you should cancel immediately.
- Furthermore, if you think that the card company mis-sold the insurance in the first place, you can complain. If it failed to explain the policy and the limitations on the benefits offered by the policy, you complain to the card company in the first instance. If it refuses a refund, you can appeal to the financial ombudsman service. It can order the card company to refund all your premiums (see pages 197-203).

The potential cost of a credit card PPI

Policy provider	Cost per £100 of outstanding balance	% of balance covered	Cost per £100 of monthly benefit being paid	Total additional payment with PPI
Independent broker	65p	10%	£6.50	£100
Egg	75p	10%	£7.50	£100
Barclaycard	79p	10%	£7.90	£100
Virgin	72p	3%	£24.00	£30
Morgan Stanley	76p	3%	£25.33	£30
Goldfish	78p	3%	£26.00	£30

Source: Paymentcare.co.uk

 For information on PPI relating to loans and mortgages, see pages 85-6 and 95.

Income protection insurance

If you fall ill or are made redundant, you want to know your life will not fall apart. You want the mortgage and any other bills paid that could spell disaster if there is no money available. For some years, the problem has been that private insurance cover has proved costly and hard to claim when things do go wrong. Despite the bad publicity, however, an estimated 18 million individual policies are covering mortgages, loans and credit cards in Britain at the moment. Critics of payment protection policies say they work for the lender and not the borrower. The lender can make irresponsible lending decisions knowing that the customer, and not them, has taken out insurance to cover the payments.

There are, however, other types of insurance, specifically income protection insurance, that cover a portion of your income and put you in charge of your recovery plan. It usually runs for a year and you dictate what it is used for. If bought from an independent broker, it can prove a better option than PPI, which remains hugely costly considering each policy covers just one product.

Nevertheless, you should always be wary. You may not need an income protection policy either. If you are covered at work for sickness absence and have a strong prospect of another job if you lose your current one, then you could put the money in a savings plan for when the sickness or unemployment strike.

Here are some figures to illustrate how much income protection insurance can cost for a 30-year-old customer.

- The insurance premium is more costly the older you become. For 18-25 year olds, cover is available at only £2.75 per £100 of cover.
- The policy will pay up to £1,000 or 50 per cent of a policyholder's gross monthly income, whichever is the smaller.

Provider	Rate per £100
Britishinsurance.com	£3.40
Pay Protect	£3.49
Post Office	£4.50
Paymentcare	£5.50
Insurety	£10.37

Source: Britishinsurance.com July 2007

how sales staff often mis-sell the insurance. Almost 18 million people have one kind of payment protection policy or another and most of them will never make a claim or will find they are ineligible for a payout.

If you are anxious about covering interest payments on your debts, you should instead consider an income protection policy sold by an insurance broker (see box, opposite).

Don't take out a credit card loan

It is a rare credit card holder that has not been sent letters or received telephone calls from their credit card provider offering additional 'benefits', such as a loan. A loan is a better option for a credit card company because it locks you into making regular payments until the loan is paid off. However, the option of switching to a cheaper card is then lost, as is the option of paying off the debt when you feel like it. You must keep up the payments each month, just like any other loan.

In fact, you should try to avoid these offers. First, they are what the marketing consultants call a 'distressed purchase' – precisely because you face rising debts and are in distress. The card company suspects this because you are already in debt with them. It hopes you trust they will seek to solve the problem as quickly and painlessly as possible.

But buying financial products on impulse is just as bad as impulse buying anything else:

- **You don't make a rational decision** based on a few moments quiet consideration.
- **You don't compare costs** with other lenders.

And yet you sign up for a three- or five-year commitment that will cost a lot of money to break.

Second, the card companies charge more for their loans than specialist loan providers. At the time of going to press, it was still possible to get a loan from a high street bank for an interest rate of 6.9 per cent compared to the 10 per cent plus loan rates of the credit card providers.

Shopping around, something you have already heard much about in this book and will hear some more in forthcoming chapters, is essential to avoid being ripped off.

Don't withdraw cash on a credit card

Credit card providers will send literature with card bills telling you how you can use their cards to withdraw cash at cash points. It is convenient, the adverts say, to have another way to withdraw cash in addition to having a debit card to access money from a bank account. However, you should be aware that any money you

❝ Credit card loans are rarely a good deal and should be avoided.❞

withdraw in this way is added to your credit card debt. The interest rate is usually 2 per cent or 2.5 per cent a month, which is up to 30 per cent a year. Some also charge a fee for cash withdrawals.

Attempts to pay the debt incurred by cash withdrawals and their associated higher interest rates will prove futile. All other balances with the card provider must be paid off first before you can start reducing that particular part of your debt. As a solution, however temporary, to debt problems it must be rejected.

Don't use credit card cheques

Credit card cheques are just like other cheques and have gained in popularity among people who need to pay builders and other tradesman without dipping into their bank account. But they come with a sky-high interest rate, which is charged at the same rate as a credit card loan, making these offers a bad deal and best avoided.

Such cheques have caused huge controversy among debt campaigners and MPs. Many campaigners believe they are a temptation put in the path of the least well off and least well-educated consumers of financial services. Which? has campaigned for tighter regulations over who receives them and how they are sold. Some credit card companies have voluntarily reviewed their policies, but many others continue to pester their customers with unwanted credit card chequebooks.

CHANGING PROVIDER

Credit card companies, like all financial firms, spend millions of pounds attracting new customers and to pay for it milk their existing customers. It shouldn't be the case, but few firms reward loyalty. They are only too happy to take you for granted. Switching, in this environment, pays off.

Your ability to switch provider is largely down to your credit score (see pages 42–5). If you have realised there is a problem with your finances before defaulting on any loans or leaving bills unpaid, your score should still be high. A high credit score will allow you to switch to most credit cards on offer without too much trouble and so benefit from their introductory offers. Before contacting a new credit card company:

- **Add up your bill.** Most card providers will ask for a list of debts to be transferred and the type of cards you use (Visa or Mastercard).
- **Look for a better deal** so that you pay less each month in interest than at the moment. Whether you have a £1,000 or £10,000 balance on your card, it will be worth switching if you can.
- **Look for as low a transfer fee charge as possible** (see pages 53–4). It is getting harder to find a card that does not impose a balance transfer fee, though there are still a few providers that don't.

‟ Credit card cheques allow you to pay bills without dipping into your current account, but they offer a bad deal that is best avoided. **”**

Case Study   Peter and Jane

Peter and Jane have two credit cards, each with a balance of £5,000. They have recently switched to new card providers. Peter has chosen an interest-free introductory offer for 12 months with a 3 per cent signing-on fee. Jane has opted for a lifetime balance transfer offer that fixes her interest at 5.9 per cent until it is paid off. Both Peter and Jane go shopping and pay £100 each for different items with their credit cards.

Despite Peter spending £150 signing up for his credit card he finds that his £100 of spending is now charged at the standard rate of 17.9 per cent a year rather than the 0 per cent he was expecting. He pays an extra £100 at the end of the month only to find that it reduces only some of the debt in the introductory offer rather than reducing the whole bill, and consequently some of the debt that is being charged at 17.9 per cent. He rings the card provider's call centre to be told that he must pay off all the debt from the introductory offer before he can start reducing the £100 charged at the standard rate. His mistake is costly. He must either pay £17.90 a year on the £100 debt, or switch again to another provider, probably incurring another £150 signing-on fee.

Jane has the same problem. Her £100 of extra spending is also charged at 17.9 per cent. The difference is that unlike Peter she wasn't thinking of switching to another provider anytime soon. Her decision to opt for the lifetime deal meant she was already paying some interest. For that reason she failed to notice a small increase in her monthly interest bill. Not until later did she see her mistake.

Again, the only way to actually stop paying the standard interest rate on the £100 was for Jane to switch provider again.

Check the maths first

The advent of balance transfer fees means that if you are switching cards to benefit from a 0 per cent offer, you might end up worse off than if you had kept the debt on your existing card. The cost of borrowing on a card with a 0 per cent balance transfer period of six months and a 2.5 per cent fee is effectively an annual equivalent interest rate of 8.9 per cent. If the fee is 3 per cent, it would be 10.7 per cent.

In answer to this problem, several companies offer what they call 'lifetime balances'. They will transfer your debt and put it in an account that charges interest at anywhere between 3.9 per cent and 6.9 per cent. If you believe you will have the self-discipline to leave the card alone, then it can be a much cheaper way to keep debt than continuing to suffer standard credit card interest of anywhere between 13.9 per cent to 20.9 per cent.

You can't keep switching

Two or three years ago there was an epidemic of credit card switching. The credit card companies were cutting each other's throats to get new customers. Many were offering 12 months interest-free cards on balance transfers and purchases to get to the top of 'best buy' tables.

Those days have gone, though. Credit card companies are more circumspect and they are looking for customers that will make them money. They therefore pay closer attention to an applicant's credit scores before making offers of interest-free cards.

Your credit score will record each time you switch provider. If you look like a regular switcher, credit card providers will start to refuse your application. Refusals will then be lodged on your credit record. When you hunt for an alternative card, your applications will also be recorded and the more applications you make, the more they will suspect you are simply after the best deal and will leave for another 'best buy' offer six months later. At this point you could run out of options and will be forced to look for an unsecured loan or an increase in your mortgage to stop you defaulting interest repayments.

❝ The days of the credit card regular switcher are gone. Providers are looking for customers who will make money for them. ❞

Dealing with credit card debt

When your credit card debt starts to build, it is time to take swift action to stop it getting out of hand. Continuing your old spending habits while debts get bigger can be like an addiction that leads you to go in search of yet more credit. Without realising it, your desire to maintain a certain lifestyle and meet large monthly minimum payment commitments are making matters much worse.

There are three types of credit card holders who retain a balance at the end of each month. Depending on what type of user you are, there are different things you can do to help keep your debt in check. But first of all, here is advice on good general practice to keep your credit card debt in as good shape as possible:

- **Set up a direct debit** when you sign up. A direct debit will make sure you pay at least the minimum sum each month.
- **Write a note in your diary** as a reminder one month before the end of any introductory offers. This will give you adequate time to switch the debt to another card or switch it to another form of debt, such as a loan or a mortgage.

❝ Control your credit cards – don't let them control you. ❞

LOW-MAINTENANCE CREDIT CARD USERS

Some people simply forget to pay before the end of their interest-free period or spend a bit above their budget. These will clear their balance at the next opportunity. It might be one month, it might be three, but it won't be long. If this is you, then there's nothing more you can do to keep your credit card spending habits under control.

LARGE CREDIT CARD BALANCES

This group keep large credit card balances to benefit from low or zero interest rate offers. Some people have been known to keep £40,000 or more on a rotating wheel of credit cards, all offering interest-free credit for between six months and a year.

If you fall into this category, you have benefited from some of the cheapest credit around, yet you could still be heading for trouble when the companies put the brakes on cheap borrowing. It might seem obvious to say that credit card companies are not charities and want to make the most profit they can, but cut-price offers over the last ten years have lulled all of us into a false sense of their charity. Costs are going up and credit cards are becoming more expensive to use.

If this is you, here are some ways you can help keep your balance as controlled as possible.

Look for the card that best suits your needs

Do you want to switch a balance or spend? You might want two cards, one doing each task. For instance, most card providers demand significant repayments each month. If you have a £5,000 debt on a card, even without interest payments, the card provider will want you to pay off at least £100 a month. If that leaves you stretched, you could also apply for a card that charges 0 per cent interest on purchases.

If you spend £100 a month on the card used for purchases and both cards have the same interest-free period, say six months, your purchase card debt will be 6 x £100 = £600.

Meanwhile, you will have reduced the balance on your balance transfer card by 6 x £100 = £600, leaving the remaining balance at £4,400. The total debt remains at £5,000.

There are many deals available at any one time and it pays to research which one will best suit you. But if you are in debt, you should aim to get the ones that charge the least interest.

Always set up a direct debit when you apply for a card

This will prevent you missing a payment during the interest-free period. It is important because if you miss a payment deadline, the card company will cut off your introductory offer and switch you to its higher standard interest rate. If this happens to you, call the card company as soon as you realise and ask for the offer period to remain in place. Negotiation at the earliest possible moment is always the best policy.

> **❝ The cut-price deals of the past offer false security: costs are going up and credit cards are expensive to use. ❞**

 For more advice on switching cards, go to the Which? website at www.which.co.uk and search for 'credit cards'. There is also a section on FAQs and how to beat identity fraud.

CREDIT CARD USERS WHO ARE OUT OF CONTROL

This is the group of credit card users who have reached the end of their tether. They can't pay off balances and struggle to pay the interest on the credit card(s). They have run out of money and run out of credit elsewhere. To prevent themselves defaulting on the loan, they need to arrest the situation and take action.

If this is you, the first step must be to cut up the cards to stop your spending habit. Then sit down and gather together all the information you need to make the best of a bad situation.

Then you need to assess whether your credit card debts are your only outstanding financial liability. Debt advisers always stress the need to deal with all financial problems and not just those that seem easier to sort out. If you also have a large overdraft or an unsecured loan or a mortgage, you need to go back to basics with the debt management plan on pages 136–8.

If credit card debt is your main problem

You must first gather together your credit card statement(s) and add up the total debt. Check the statement(s) for:

- The latest figure(s) on your balance.
- The size of the next monthly payment(s).
- What interest rate you are paying. Not all card companies include this information. If you cannot see it, call the card company and ask for the information.

If you are paying the standard interest rate, typically 17–18 per cent, the first move is to see if you can switch to a cheaper provider (see pages 60–2).

If you haven't yet missed a monthly repayment Your credit score should still be good, but some card providers will reject you because your income is too small in relation to your debt position. Others will be less concerned.

Verdict: Switching to another card provider should be relatively simple (see pages 60–2). Walk into a high street bank or building society and ask to switch your balance. Alternatively, use a telephone or internet-based broking service. A broker will have access to hundreds of card deals. You don't pay a fee because they earn their money from the finance company you pick from their list.

Add any fee to your balance and begin the process of repairing your finances without a card company breathing down your neck.

If you have started missing repayments Your credit score will begin to plummet once you miss repayments. Most card companies will forgive one missed repayment if you promise to start making repayments again. But further missed payments will harm your credit record and be a significant bar on switching to a cheaper card provider.

At this stage, you need to negotiate with your creditors. Use the debt management plan (pages 136–8) to assess your income and outgoings and to decide how much you can afford to pay. If it is clear that you will be unable to pay other bills if you continue keeping the credit card company happy, there is no point kidding yourself or them that you are going to be able to keep your finances under control for much longer.

Remember, though, that credit card debt is classified as a 'non-priority' debt (see page 19). You can't be imprisoned for your inability to pay non-priority debts and you are unlikely to lose your home or its contents. It doesn't matter if you are unable to pay because of changed circumstances or because in a weak moment you spent money you couldn't afford to repay.

 Most debt advisers reckon you must have at least £100 of disposable income that you can use to make repayments if your debts are larger than £5,000. Without that £100, you will need to consider more drastic action.

If you genuinely don't have any income to spare for repayments, the credit card company must then talk to you on that basis.

Ask the expert

What if the debt has passed to debt collectors?

When card companies sell on your debt to debt collectors, it is because the card company has decided it is not cost-effective for them to pursue the debt. That is usually because you haven't contacted the lender to explain your situation. They write you off and sell the problem on to a specialist. In most cases, card companies, like other unsecured creditors, only expect to receive between 5p and 10p in the £1 from a debt collector.

It is an offence under the Administration of Justice Act 1970 (among others) for someone in debt to be harassed by their creditor, such as a credit card company or an agent acting on their behalf. Debts of under £5,000 can only be heard at the small claims court. So even if you do get taken to court, you can't be stung with solicitors' costs if you lose.

Debt collectors are not the same as bailiffs (see pages 172–5). Debt collectors cannot take any action against you, apart from asking you to pay any money owed. Regardless of what they say, you don't have to let debt collectors into your home. They are not allowed to force their way in unless you have let them in on a previous visit, hence the importance of never, ever letting them in.

Loans

Finance companies advertise a bewildering array of loans just about everywhere you look. Almost every bank statement comes with the offer of a loan and a message urging you to embark on a spending spree. In the words of one advert, taking out a loan allows you to 'buy your dreams'. However, for many people, a loan is less about realising a dream than keeping their head above water.

Types of loan

In this chapter we discuss the different types of loans that are available together with other forms of loan debt, like hire purchase. We examine how they work and what you can do to manage them better. Once they are under control, you can budget and get on top of your finances.

For the purposes of this book, loans are separated into two main types – **personal loans** and **secured loans**. They involve different methods of borrowing money, but are often advertised in a way that one is confused for the other.

Some loans can be secured, others **unsecured**. You need to find out exactly what you are getting into. The main difference is that lenders offering you a secured loan want a guarantee that they will get their money back if you can no

Jargon buster

Consolidation loan If you have multiple debts with different lenders – on credit cards, loans, with friends and family – you can shift them all to a single loan, known as a consolidation loan. You can consolidate debts in a personal loan or an unsecured loan

Personal loan A fixed amount of money borrowed from a bank or other lender. Usually unsecured (see below) and can be used to pay for holidays, cars, weddings, etc. Can also be used to consolidate other debts from credit cards and other loans (not mortgages). The usual term of the loan is three or five years. The maximum is ten years

Secured loan A fixed amount of money borrowed from a specialist lender. The

loan guarantees the lender it will get its money back if you can no longer afford the payments. Usually your home will be used as security for the loan. If you already have a mortgage, it will be the equivalent of a second mortgage. The usual term of such a loan is 10–30 years

Unsecured loan Can be a fixed or flexible amount of money borrowed from a bank, specialist lender or other finance company. The loan is based on a contract with the lender. If you breach the contract, the lender can pursue you through the courts for the debt. Several other types of loan are unsecured. An overdraft or credit card balance is, in effect, a flexible, unsecured loan

longer afford the payments. If you offer your home as a guarantee, they know they can force a sale to pay off the loan. Your home is not the only security you can offer – some lenders accept your car or expensive jewellery – but it is the most common.

Personal loans are usually unsecured. You are not offering any security. The lender believes it will get its money back because you have signed a contract that can be enforced through the courts. They know that if you break the contract, it can seriously harm your credit history.

Consolidation loans are the latest type of loan to hit the market. The problem for borrowers is that they are marketed as an unsecured loan when most of them require you to guarantee to pay it back by putting your home up as security (see page 73 for more on consolidation loans).

PERSONAL LOANS

Personal loans remain popular because they are simple to arrange and allow consumers to budget their spending over a few years to buy an expensive item, such as a kitchen, a wedding or something like a special holiday. In the last decade, when inflation and interest rates have remained low, personal loans have also remained cheap.

If you are a homeowner with a good credit history, a successful application can result in a large lump sum being paid into your bank account within a few days. The fact that they are so simple to get hold of is one of the reasons why so many people have a personal loan. If you can get the advertised interest rate – often between 6 and 7 per cent (2007) – you have a means of borrowing at little more than mortgage interest.

Nevertheless, how much you can borrow and how much it will cost in monthly instalments will, as with so much lending, depend on your credit score (see pages 42–5). Some surveys have concluded that as many as one in four adults in the UK have a credit history that gives lenders pause for thought. An unpaid bill or series of late payments and penalty fines can give you what the industry calls an 'impaired credit history'. If you are in this position, shopping around can just hurt your credit rating further.

In the first instance, whether you rent or own your home, you should ask for quotes for loans rather than making applications. Lenders will look at your credit history before responding to an application and this will only leave a 'footprint' on your credit file that other lenders can see. Most lenders will not look kindly on someone shopping around for a loan and being turned down (see page 62).

If this tactic fails, a renter may be forced to take more drastic action or borrow from elsewhere (friends or family). If you are a homeowner, you may find the only route to reasonably priced borrowing lies in the direction of a secured loan (see pages 71–2).

A personal (unsecured) loan has advantages over other forms of lending.

- **It is short-term,** which allows you to pay off the debt in a few years rather than decades.
- **It is a fixed monthly payment,** which allows you to budget.
- **It is unsecured,** so you avoid the need to put up security for the loan.
- **There are low interest rates** available. The intense level of competition in the loan industry on headline interest rates means you can get a low rate deal.

The typical APR of a personal loan can range from 6 to almost 35 per cent. A repayment term starts from six months and will usually last three to five years. Sums borrowed range from £1,000 up to £25,000. Maximum borrowing is £25,000 and the maximum time for re-paying the loan is up to ten years.

Some finance companies will sell loans in different flavours, such as the wedding loan, the tenant loan and the home improvement loan. There is even the bad credit loan. As a car enthusiast would say, when you look under the bonnet these loans are much the same. The only major difference is the interest rate, which is largely governed by your credit score.

❝ At least half of the new cars bought in Britain are financed by a loan from the bank, manufacturer or a third-party company. ❞

Types of personal (unsecured) loan

Probably the most traditional unsecured loan is the car loan. At least half of new cars that are bought in Britain are paid for with a loan, either from the manufacturer, a bank loan or a third-party finance company.

They work like the bulk of unsecured loans. You agree a term, usually three or five years. After a credit check, the loan company offers an interest rate and a monthly payment is agreed. The loan itself will come with a couple of pages of very small print setting out the terms of the agreement.

Consumers commonly commit anything between £100 and £500 a month to purchasing a car with a loan. Many will consider it a fixed element of their monthly outgoings that never goes away. They sell the car after say, three years, and use the proceeds as a deposit on a new car purchase. Every three years the process is repeated.

You can ask for flexibility in your loan terms in case you want to pay the loan early or vary payments over the term of the loan, though that will add to the expense. The ability to pay off the loan early, a flexible interest rate and the ability to take **repayment holidays** are popular. Some lenders will bow to the demands, though not always and usually only if you have an unblemished credit history.

A loan company can only offer low interest rates if it knows the deal is fixed for a set period and for a set amount each month.

SECURED LOANS

A secured loan is subject to the Consumer Credit Act 1974. The Act contains strict regulations about how money is lent and covers loans up to a value of £25,000. There is a seven-day consideration period given to allow time for you to assess the implications of the credit agreement.

Lenders offering secured loans ask you to provide them with some form of security. In almost all cases, the security is your home, though you can use your business. If you should default on the loan, your lender goes through the Land Registry to place a legal right on your home. In the pecking order of creditors, a lender of a secured loan takes second place to a mortgage lender, so if the home is repossessed and sold, the lender would get their money back only when the mortgage had been paid off.

A secured loan can be for a much higher sum than an unsecured loan – from £5,000 to £50,000, or in some cases as much as £130,000, says data provider Moneyfacts. They are usually for more than £30,000. To keep repayments low, lenders increase the term of the loan, which can run for 25 years. This prevents huge monthly payments from taking all the household's disposable income, though, as a result, the total debt is greater and can be more

than double the amount you borrowed. Most loans will have extra charges for early repayment.

The amount you can borrow, the term available and the interest rate all depend upon the equity you have in your property, the lender's view of your ability to repay the loan and your personal

Money management tip

Secured loans offer poor value for money. If possible, it is always better to borrow more on your existing mortgage to repay debts or fund home improvements. If you cannot borrow more on your mortgage, then you could be spending more of your disposable income on debt than you probably should. Mortgage lenders tend to only refuse applications when you have reached a reasonable credit limit. Instead of increasing your debts further, you need to address your financial situation more seriously (see pages 14–27).

❝ There is a seven-day consideration period to allow you to assess the credit implications. ❞

Rather than taking out a secured loan, some people choose to re-mortgage their property – for more information on this subject, see pages 101-5.

circumstances, for example any adverse credit. Subject to your circumstances, you may be able to borrow up to 125 per cent of the property value.

Secured homeowner loans are available in varying amounts and for many different purposes, including debt consolidation.

Charging orders

A secured loan can result in the loss of your home if you default although, increasingly, so can a personal loan. Lenders are using a little-known technical rule that allows them to apply for a '**charging order**', which places unsecured debt against your property. From the lender's point of view, what was once an unsecured debt suddenly has some security.

You can fight the imposition of a charging order, but it is far better not to reach that stage in your battle to keep ahead on debt repayments.

Jargon buster

Charging order A charging order is an order from the court and is placed on a debtor's property, usually his or her home, for money owed to a lender. If you have a personal loan and you have not kept to the repayment arrangement, a lender can request the court to place a charging order on your property so that when the property is sold you will have to pay that debt before any of the proceeds are given to you. In basic terms, the unsecured debt becomes secured on your property

Repayment holiday A lender can allow you to miss a payment for a month or several months. This is known as a repayment holiday. It is more common for mortgage holders to be allowed respite from monthly payments, but lenders offering personal loans and secured loans will increasingly agree to a payment holiday

Case Study   James and Judith Hughes

James and Judith Hughes took out a loan secured on their Wolverhampton home in the early 1990s for £6,000. They thought their last payment would be March 2006, but they were told by the loan company that they still owed more than £30,000 because the account fell into arrears at one point and this caused charges and interest at a daily rate.

The couple lost their home when they were forced to declare themselves bankrupt.

> **!** Interest rates on a secured loan tend to be variable, so they can go up or down at any time – something of a risk for a borrower on a tight budget. You can opt for a fixed interest rate in the same way as you can with a mortgage. A fixed rate will usually cost more. The key fact that lenders must highlight in their advertising literature is that: 'Your home is at risk if you do not keep up repayments on a mortgage or other loan secured on it.'

CONSOLIDATION LOAN

A consolidation loan is the term used for a loan that allows you to sweep up all your debts – on credit cards, loans or with friends and family – into a single loan. You can use a personal loan or an unsecured loan to do this. For some people it is merely a case of lumping together credit card debts in a personal loan. If they have a good credit history, they can consolidate their credit card bills before they get out of control. Others are tempted to consolidate when they have already lost control and believe it will make life easier having everything in one place.

If your credit history has already suffered from late payments or defaults, you will find it difficult consolidating debts on a low interest rate in a personal loan. Instead, the only place you can consolidate will be in a secured loan. Many people believe they are consolidating debts in a personal (unsecured) loan when they are, in fact, using a secured loan. They find themselves in this situation because of the misleading way many 'consolidation loans' are advertised.

Adverts for debt consolidation loans look like personal loan adverts. Even when there are prominent labels on the adverts telling the consumer they could lose their home if they fail to keep up with repayments, studies have shown people believe the only loan secured against a home is a mortgage. Debt advisers say many of the people who fall behind with repayments on a secured debt consolidation loan didn't realise their home was in jeopardy.

Most advisers recommend secured consolidation loans. They argue that consumers are increasing the risk of losing their home (because the debts brought together in the new loan are usually unsecured). There is also evidence that people who use debt consolidation loans fail to address the debts problems and discover why they are in debt (see confusion marketing, page 82). There are worrying signs that for many people a consolidation loan is but the start of their problems and not the end. Within a few months they begin spending all over again and the situation gets worse.

How repayments can stack up

The cost of a secured loan looks lower than other forms of borrowing as it is spread over a longer period of time, not because interest rates are necessarily lower. For example, a £10,000 personal loan, even at an interest rate of 15 per cent, will result in interest charges of £4,000 over five years, compared with the £22,000 interest charges on a £10,000 secured loan spread over 25 years at 12.9 per cent.

BAD CREDIT LOAN

A bad credit loan is the name some lenders use to target people with a poor credit history. If you have a bad credit history, you will score highly with a lender who is targeting defaulters and bad payers. It is usually a secured loan at a higher interest rate than a standard unsecured loan. The lender will accept you on the basis that the threat of losing your house will make you more disciplined when making repayments in the future.

ANNUAL PERCENTAGE RATE (APR)

It is the APR quoted by the lender that will effect how much you need to repay each month. However, the quoted APR acts only as a guide as the exact rate offered will be on an individual basis and according to your credit history.

Lenders will apply their own credit scoring rules to your credit history and decide if you are a good risk or not. They must offer the advertised rate to at least two-thirds of the people who successfully apply for a loan. As a general rule, it is advisable to compare the APRs of different loans, as this is a good way to determine how competitive they are.

Case Study Simon and Anne Jones

Debt advisers based in the northwest tried to help Simon and Anne Jones when they contacted them to talk about their growing problem with loans. They had had a series of small loans with a single lender and were told that they could have a bigger loan because they were house owners. They signed a new agreement for £20,000 unaware that this was secured on their home. The APR was 27 per cent, which meant that over the full term of the loan they would be paying back over £50,000. There didn't seem to be anything that could be done about the way the loan was sold and the fact that the couple were unaware it was secured because they had both signed the agreement and a charging order. The couple were at risk of losing their home, as they could no longer afford the repayments. However, the debt advisers argued the secured loan agreement may be unenforceable due to the way it had been set out. A court case is still pending.

Personal (unsecured) versus secured loans

The similarities

- They are less flexible. A penalty charge will be applied to the loan if you repay your loan earlier than agreed, miss a payment or apply to extend the loan beyond the agreed date
- They can limit your ability to get the best mortgage deal or other credit. The more you borrow to fund your general spending or to pay off old loans, the less headroom you will have for borrowing on your mortgage. It means that when you come to move house, both secured and unsecured loans will limit the size of mortgage you can expect and therefore limit the size of house you can buy
- They come with a higher rate of interest if you fail to satisfy credit-scoring criteria

The differences

- Approval of unsecured loans can be quick. Some finance companies claim they can process a claim in minutes. Secured loans need information verifying that you own your home. As well as the usual credit scoring, lenders will also check that the size of your current mortgage doesn't prohibit borrowing more money
- Technically, tenants can apply for unsecured loans. As long as your job appears to be secure and your income enough to pay monthly instalments, the loan is available. However, recent evidence shows this is less and less the case. Lenders are raising the bar all the time for tenants, who are finding it harder and harder to get unsecured debt
- Crucially, an unsecured loan avoids the risk of home repossession. There are no ties, but the lender does have a contract, which they can take to court. If the court upholds the contract, the lender can pursue you with bailiffs (see pages 172–5). A secured lender can also obtain court orders and use bailiffs to repay the debt. But the secured lender has the added benefit of security, which provides protection in the event of a customer's inability to repay. An unsecured lender can apply for a charging order on your property, but cannot use this, except in extreme circumstances, to trigger repossession of your home
- Secured loans can be offered to the self-employed and people who have recently changed jobs, moved house or who have adverse credit
- Secured loans are also useful for larger amounts stretched over a longer repayment period, unlike personal loans, which are generally smaller sums repaid over a short period

Debt and the economy

The number of loans available and how many people take them on has risen steeply in the last ten years. So much so, that many economists describe us as a nation hooked on short-term debt. Traditionally, short-term loans were a popular way for millions of people to buy cars and furniture. Today, they are used to fund just about every type of purchase and form the backbone of short-term lending in the UK.

The 1990s witnessed an unprecedented boom in the amount of unsecured debt. Britons began to borrow like they had never borrowed before. It fuelled a ten-year consumer-driven economic boom, but also posed the question, 'Will there be a terrible hangover?' That question remains unanswered.

In recent years, the doomsayers have appeared overly pessimistic. Each year they say there will be a crash, but the crash never comes. Yet the debts have piled up. Unsecured borrowing has increased as a proportion of our national income and is getting bigger and bigger. In 1995, unsecured borrowing accounted for 15 per cent of national income. By 2006, it had risen to 24 per cent.

The rise indicates that UK consumer borrowing has increased at a faster rate than earnings and productivity. That didn't matter while borrowing money was cheap, with interest rates at historic lows. Borrowing is still relatively cheap, but who knows if that will continue.

> ❝ Goods bought with a loan or credit card belong to you straightaway, unlike those paid by hire purchase. ❞

LOAN-TYPE AGREEMENTS

Loan-type agreements such as **hire purchase** (HP) and **conditional sale agreements** are making a comeback. As the criteria tighten on unsecured loans, people of all incomes are turning to HP as a way to buy. This is because the companies who offer HP agreements rely less on credit scoring than other lenders. Popular with car owners, they are now gaining ground as a way to buy furniture, a new kitchen and white goods.

When you buy using a loan or credit card, the goods belong to you straightaway. When you buy with hire purchase or conditional sale agreement, you don't legally own the goods until you've paid back all the money you owe.

How they work

Under an HP or conditional sale agreement, you pay an initial deposit followed by monthly payments over an agreed period. The monthly payments consist of a portion of the money you borrowed plus the interest. At the end of the agreed period, you have the option of owning the goods outright. With an HP agreement, the lender may require you to pay a fee before the goods are yours. A conditional sale agreement works in the same way as an HP loan, although you will not be required to pay a fee at the end. The limitations to these forms of loan are:

- Buyers cannot modify or sell goods purchased with an HP agreement without the lender's permission, until they are owned outright.

- **Your contract is with the finance company** who provide the HP, not the retailer, and it is the finance company that will own the goods until the final payment is made.
- **If you fail to keep up with the payments,** it is possible for a creditor to repossess the goods, although they cannot steal them back if you have already paid a third of the credit price of the goods. If they want their goods returned, they will have to take you to court and apply for a return order. The county court will send you a form (N9C) with the claim that you should return if you want the court to suspend the return of goods order and allow you to keep the goods. You also need to offer to pay the debt back in monthly instalments you can afford.
- **Although once a third of the bill is paid** you can terminate the deal, there may be penalty clauses that you should watch out for.
- **You are liable for any damage** caused to the goods during the contract period.

Read the small print

HP contracts should set out in plain English what you are expected to pay and when. Agreements for purchases of less than £25,000 that do not include all the important financial information may be difficult for the lender to enforce. In fact, they may have to resort to a court order to get you to comply.

As with all other loan agreements, if you have any questions, ask your lender or, in the case of HP, ask the retailer. If you are still unsure, seek independent advice before committing yourself. Don't sign anything you don't understand.

You may be offered payment protection insurance to cover you against ill health or unemployment. If you are buying a car, you may also be offered guaranteed asset protection insurance (GAP) to cover you against any shortfall on your own motor insurance if the car is written off or stolen. In both cases, the insurance is not worth taking out (see the payment protection insurance box, page 85).

Personal contract purchase

Like HP, a personal contract purchase (PCP) is an increasingly popular way to buy a car. A PCP allows you to pay for a car in instalments and buy it outright at the end of the contract term. It has become popular because it protects buyers from negative equity, a particular problem when second-hand car prices fall off a cliff. If the total payments at the end of the term are more than the car is worth, you can put the difference in value into a new car purchase. In this way, you can recycle the negative equity into your next PCP deal rather than pay a final instalment on a car worth much less than predicted.

The downside is cost. Most experts believe you pay more over the longer term for this protection against negative equity. Furthermore, if you get into financial difficulties midway through a contract, you will have a problem. Just like HP agreements, the goods belong to the seller until the last payment is made. You can try to negotiate, but experience tells us that car finance companies are not the most lenient when it comes to negotiation. The loan company cannot steal your car back if you have paid more than a third of the credit price. Instead, as with the rules governing HP, the lender will need to take you to court.

STUDENT LOANS

There are tens of thousands of former higher education students with debts dating back to their college days. At the moment, the average college student graduates with about £16,000 of debts. Students starting college last year under a new scheme of tuition fees will leave weighed down by an estimated £30,000 of debt. That's not a made-up figure – it is agreed by both the National Union of Students (NUS) and the Department for Education. They say that average debts from now on will be at least £10,000 a year.

Partly the rise is due to the introduction of a £3,070-a-year tuition fee in 2006. Partly it is the jump in housing costs faced by students, especially in London and the big metropolitan centres. The government says it has eased the pain by increasing tuition loans to match the rise in fees. It has also brought in maintenance loans to keep students out of the clutches of credit card companies and loan sharks.

Unfortunately, living costs don't stand still. Rising bills for items like gas and electricity have added to the burden, which means that overdrafts, credit card balances and bank loans remain part of most students' debt pile.

There are full maintenance grants available to students from low-income families. These are worth £2,800. The

Maintenance loans

Student maintenance loans have increased to an annual maximum of £6,315 in London, £4,510 elsewhere and to £5,375 for those that stray overseas. Students living at their parents' home in London or elsewhere get £3,495. They are available from the Student Loans Company (SLC), which manages all student loans.

Compared to high street lenders, student debt is cheap. Interest isn't added to the loan until further education is completed and then the rate of interest is linked to inflation (the retail price index (RPI)) and not the Bank of England base rate. In 2006, that meant the rate was 2.4 per cent. During the year, the Bank of England raised rates to 5 per cent, pushing commercial interest loans much higher than student maintenance loans.

 The Student Loans Company (SLC) is a UK public sector organisation that provides loans and grants to students in colleges and universities England, Northern Ireland, Scotland and Wales. To find out more, go to www.slc.co.uk.

government plans to increase the number of students who qualify for these grants by 50,000 in September 2008 with a £400 million funding boost for the scheme. More than 250,000 students from lower income families will also get higher levels of maintenance grant. Students from families with incomes of up to £25,000 a year will be entitled to full grants, up from £17,500 in 2007. Those whose families have incomes of up to £60,000 will be entitled to some grant, up from £37,000 in 2007.

Graduates will also be able to take a 'repayment holiday' on their loans for up to five years to give them financial space to buy a home or start a family.

Repayments

Calculating repayments over time on the government portion of the debt is tricky. The rule is that you pay 9 per cent of what you earn over £15,000 per year, £1,250 per month or £288 per week. Therefore, a job paying £20,000 a year before tax will trigger a deduction of 9 per cent on £5,000, which is £450 a year or £37.50 a month. The NUS says a student loan that reached £20,000 will take 22 years to pay off given a 'typical graduate salary profile'. A

Money management tip

If you have still got a financial hangover from university days, banks debts are the ones to tackle first.

£15,000 debt will take just over 16 years to clear.

If you have a student loan, the SLC will advise the tax authority, HMRC, when your salary reaches the level that requires you to start repaying the loan. HMRC, in turn, instruct your employer to deduct repayments from your gross income. The SLC sends an annual statement about the level of your debt to you for your information, which you need to keep with other records of debts.

False consciousness

Student loans are often talked about as if they are free money to be paid back some time in the distant future. It appears like free money at the beginning because interest is not applied to the loan until after you have left college. The cheap interest rate has also encouraged some people to see a money-making opportunity. There are plenty of recent stories in the newspapers of wealthy parents taking their children's entitlement to student loans and re-investing it at a higher interest rate. After their child leaves college they pay back the loan, making a profit on the three years of savings interest, minus, of course, the student loan interest.

To the not-so-wealthy, these three years of free interest paint a distorted picture. The interest is simply deferred and added to the total debt. Like any compounded interest, this soon adds up and by graduation the debt may be much bigger than expected. (For more information about compound interest see page 41.)

Hardship grants/loans

Also known as access funds, hardship loans are available through college from the government. They were set up to assist students who are in serious financial difficulty. There are many hurdles to jump before you can get an extra loan, but generally if you can prove you are in need of financial assistance, you could receive a lump sum of up to £500 cash. If you receive hardship funds in the form of a loan, it will be added to your student loan account and will have to be paid back in the same way. Grants, however, don't have to be paid back.

Colleges also often have their own hardship funds of around £100, which will pay a utility bill or other emergency payment if necessary.

If you are experiencing trouble paying bills while at college, it is worth claiming these loans. Each college will have its own rules and the administrator handling claims should be sympathetic. As a basic rule, you will need an overdraft of at least £500 and some evidence that you have bills you cannot pay without racking up more debt.

Claiming the loans will have no impact on your credit score, but failing to pay bills and defaulting on commercial loans will harm your ability to borrow in the future.

❝Students who prove they are in serious financial difficulty could get a cash sum of up to £500. Loans must be repaid, unlike grants.❞

If you need a loan

There are more than 1,000 finance companies offering loans and online brokers offer a wide range of deals. To find out more, newspaper personal finance sections give the current best buys (usually a top ten list of the best offers) (see page 100).

MAKING YOUR CHOICE

Which? has long argued that only a tiny minority of people should opt for a secured loan. The Consumer Credit Counselling Service says secured loans offer an appropriate solution for about 3 per cent of over-indebted people, 'but the adverts imply they are appropriate for the majority'.

There are plenty of people who feel they're in a financial fix and make a judgement that a secured loan is the only option. They might have recently bought a home and be locked into a three- or five-year mortgage deal. They have an unsecured loan already, some credit card debts and an overdraft. They make a judgement that a secured loan is their only salvation when they discover large repairs are needed on the home, a relative is in financial trouble or they lose their job and want some cash to tide them over until they find work again. But while these seem like sound reasons for extending credit levels, there are huge dangers.

- A study by one broker found that secured loans are lasting on average no more than three years. That's because lenders are encouraging people who already have a consolidation loan and have run out of credit, to trade in the loan for a bigger one.
- This loan will probably stretch over a longer timescale to keep the monthly payments as low as possible. Yet it will almost certainly fail to solve the problem.
- Banks and other major lenders offer you the option of talking to them in branch offices, over the telephone, by written application or online through their website. If you have access to the web, whether at

 If you have debts that are far beyond the capacity of your income, then you need to do something more radical. See pages 144-66.

Case Study Jeff and Rachel Brignall

Jeff and Rachel Brignall were struggling to afford repayments of £500 per month on a second mortgage when they went to debt advisers. The couple had two teenage children still at home and were living on £280 per week from Jeff's job. Rachel had been trying to get work but hadn't found anything yet and they had been struggling financially on one low income. They had council tax arrears, which had then been passed to bailiffs. They shouldn't have been able to take out a second mortgage, i.e. a second secured loan, when they already had a mortgage of £70,000 on a house valued at £72,000. Little or no check was made on their ability to repay a second loan and the couple were in danger of losing their home.

home or at a local library or internet café, try to familiarise yourself with rival loan offerings. It is one of the quickest ways to get a sense of the rates and terms and conditions.

> **❝ Taking out a secured loan is a high risk decision:** your monthly repayment fee is even larger, which means it can be even more difficult to pay off your debts. **❞**

CONFUSION MARKETING

There is evidence that many people who take out secured loans sign the contract without realising the implications. They say they were unaware their borrowing put a second charge on their home. They say they believed the loan was an ordinary personal loan and unsecured and argue, often in court after they have defaulted on loan repayments, that they would never have signed the contract if someone had told them it would jeopardise the roof over their head.

It is not hard to see how these people were unaware they were gambling with their home. The advertising and marketing literature used by lenders offering secured loans has been criticised by debt advisers as being confusing, even though adverts must legally include a phrase telling consumers that failing to make repayments could lead to the loss of their home.

Look out for this when picking a loan. If you are looking online, check the details of the loan. If you talk to staff at your bank or call a telephone-based loan company, ask if the loan is secured against your property, even if there appears to be nothing in the terms.

THE APPLICATION

Once you find a lender that seems to suit your needs you will be asked to fill in a form with some basic information about your income, employment and outgoings, how much you want to borrow and over what period. Repayments are usually made by direct debit.

Before you sign on the dotted line be sure that you ask the key questions listed below.

If you are lucky, the application will be a straightforward process, the loan approved and the money deposited in your account. However, many debt experts say adverts for personal loans are used to get you on the telephone and talking about the financial issues you

face. There is evidence that call centre staff are trained to ask about all your debts. It does not matter to them that you rang to talk about a home improvement loan or wedding loan. Your request is just the start of a conversation that, in many cases, will end with a recommendation that you consolidate all other debts in the same loan.

You may, for example, ring up for a home improvement loan. You want a conservatory on the back of your house and think a five-year home improvement loan will do the trick. The company asks you, among other things, about any other borrowings you may have and recommends you opt for a debt consolidation loan instead. More than

Ten questions to ask before taking out a loan or mortgage

1. What is the interest rate (see page 40 to find out more about how rates are calculated)?
2. Is the interest rate an introductory offer (the advertised rate may be attractive but lead to a higher rate after a few months/years)?
3. How much will I repay each month?
4. Is the interest rate variable or fixed – can the monthly payment go up or down?
5. What is the term of the loan (it may be 25 years with a mortgage, three or five years for a personal loan or six months if it is a balance transfer on a credit card)?
6. Is the loan secured or unsecured?
7. Are there any fees? This is becoming increasingly important with administration fees on mortgages going up along with fees on moving balances on credit cards. Exit fees and early redemption fees are other ones to watch.
8. Are there any penalties (sometimes called tie-ins) if, for instance, I miss payments or want to extend the life of the loan?
9. Can I vary monthly payments?
10. Are there any clauses in the small print I need to know about?

Money management tips

- **Don't borrow more than you need –** you will only spend it. And the result? You will have to pay more back in interest.
- **Can you afford the repayments?** However much you are borrowing, check what the repayments will be each month. Make sure that they won't make you overdrawn on your bank account.
- **Check the advertised interest rate.** Loan interest rates are always followed by the initials APR (annual percentage rate). The APR figures quoted in loan and credit card literature are calculated according to an agreed formula. Until recently, lenders used up to ten different methods, but the government put a stop to that.
- **Check what interest rate they offer you.** Lenders are obliged to offer two-thirds of customers the advertised rate. You need to be aware that you may be offered a higher rate according to your credit score.
- **Look at the small print.** Although the lowest APR is the main factor that contributes to a cheap loan, you should always pay attention to the small print. Penalty charges will be a factor. Some banks are worse than others at strict regulations on when to pay and how to pay. Any extra conditions will always be found in the pages marked 'terms and conditions'. Banks that offer some of the cheapest loans can be the worst offenders.
- **Check out the alternatives.** Make sure you have considered other forms of debt and whether they are better suited to your need. You may be able to get a better deal re-mortgaging. Mortgages are flexible these days and you can make overpayments without suffering penalties (see pages 88–105).
- **Only ever make one loan application at a time.** Your loan applications are recorded on your credit files and held by the three major credit reference agencies (see page 43). Multiple loan applications are frowned upon by banks, mortgage lenders and other lenders, and their records are kept for years. If you want to test the market, get a broker to get some test quotes and you will get an idea of the how much you must pay each month.
- **Always reject payment protection insurance.** The lender's sales staff will tell you if you lose your job, have an accident or become sick, monthly repayments will be covered by a payment protection policy. For most people, the policy is inappropriate (see pages 56–8). If you are concerned about the stability of your finances, consider an income protection policy instead (see page 58).

that, to get the best rate, the loan will need to be twice the size of your original estimate and secured against your home.

In another example, you apply to the lender for its 'low rate' bad credit loan. An assessment is made of your poor credit history and the application is turned down. In the next breath, you could be referred to a debt management company (see pages 130–1). The lender earns commission for each referral and the debt management company earns commission when it designs a formal structure for debt repayments. Lenders also have a sliding scale of rates – usually the larger the loan, the lower the interest rate. This policy encourages customers to take out bigger and more profitable loans.

So, when deciding on what sort of a loan would suit you best, you need to remember that loan applications have major strings attached. The sign of a good lender is that it won't carry out a credit and background check on you without your explicit agreement. Try to find a lender or broker that will give you an assessment of your ability to get a loan before using a credit rating agency. When a loan application is processed, it is registered with the credit scoring agencies Experian, Equifax and Callcredit. Each subsequent loan application will get harder as lenders notice you have made more than one application in the recent past (see also pages 42–5).

Loan payment protection insurance

On pages 56–8 we examined how credit card companies make much of their profits, not from the lending itself, but more from the sale of add-on products, like payment protection

The potential cost of a loan PPI

Compare the cost of loan protection with ten of the UK's top lenders on a £7,500 loan, with a monthly repayment of £147.33.

Lender	Rate per £100	Monthly cost of loan protection	Total cost of loan protection
Abbey	£14.29	£21.06	£1,263.60
Bank of Scotland	£40.62	£59.85	£3,591.00
HSBC	£26.29	£38.74	£2,324.40
Nationwide	£14.27	£21.03	£1,261.80
Average	£23.91	£35.22	£2,113.20

insurance (PPI). The same is the case among lenders selling personal and secured loans.

PPI is a very expensive way to buy cover for loan payments if you fall ill or are made redundant (see the box, page 85) and it is being investigated by regulators to see how this type of insurance is sold and whether there is any price fixing to keep the cost to consumers artificially high. Which? believes the sale of PPI by lenders is largely unethical and calls the whole process 'a protection racket'. Despite this, more than 18 million people are estimated to have PPI policies, and many of them have more than one.

Critics of PPI have called it the biggest mis-selling scandal of the 21st century after pensions mis-selling and endowment mortgage mis-selling in the 1990s (see page 106). Loan PPI sold by mainstream lenders, such as the banks, building societies and specialist loan providers, is probably the most expensive and least value for money of all the different types of PPI that are on the market.

The trick is that it is sold as a 'single premium' product. That means the lender will calculate the insurance needed to cover the loan payments, add it to the loan and then calculate the interest on the whole sum. For example, if you want a £7,500 loan over five years from a high street bank, the lender will add between £1,300 and £2,200 to the loan for the PPI. The interest on the loan is calculated on the whole sum, which is now almost a third bigger than the original loan. An independent insurance broker would offer the PPI for as little as £450.

Put it another way. If you want to protect monthly payments of £147.33 on a £7,500 five-year loan, you will shell out more than £1,600 than you would if you went to an independent insurance broker.

If you look at the chart on page 85 you can see that the cost is worked out per £100 of loan so you can compare providers. If you are tempted to take out PPI insurance to cover a loan (and don't be), ask for the 'cost per £100' figure to compare with buying it from an independent broker.

The other problems with loan PPI are the same as credit card PPI and mortgage PPI – that few people claim it and most of those that do are turned down by the lender. We don't have exact figures on how many people claim and how many are turned down because the banks and other lenders keep this information secret.

❝Loan PPI sold by mainstream lenders is probably the most expensive and worst value for money of all the types on the market.❞

Your property

Is re-mortgaging for you? In this chapter we look at how to get a better deal from mortgage providers to cut your outgoings and your debts. We also examine how to generate cash from your home and when to do that and when to hold back. This section also looks at dealing with rent arrears.

Mortgages

These days a mortgage can last your entire adult life, or just a few years. How long you stay with the same provider depends on how much you want to shop around for a better deal. Juggling your mortgage debt is the same as juggling credit cards and loans. They may all be different types of debt with different rules attached. Yet all are essentially the same.

HOW MORTGAGES WORK

You are loaned a certain sum of money with an interest rate and a date by which it must be repaid. You can renegotiate the deal many times, cutting the interest rate and shortening or extending the final repayment date.

This flexibility has a downside, though. An interesting study by the Consumer Credit Counselling Service (CCCS) shows that the trebling of house prices in the last ten years in many areas of the southeast has stretched the finances of a large number of middle-income families beyond breaking point. Only a few years ago, most people in debt trouble were on low incomes, usually between £10,000 and £15,000. Now, however, more people on incomes of £30,000 plus are

contacting the CCCS for advice, most of them in the capital or the surrounding counties. The CCCS believes higher mortgage payments are at the heart of the problem.

A CCCS report in 2006 said: 'While house prices have increased all over the UK, the increase has been most marked in the south. This may have led to people taking on mortgages which entail large payments to be made each month, eating away at disposable income. People may have turned to credit to bridge the gap between their incomes and their outgoings.'

Many people in the study turned to loans and credit cards to bridge the gap, many more have sought to extend their mortgages, exploiting the increase in house prices to borrow more. They are also extending the term of the mortgage. Banks and building societies have come up with a clever trick for bringing the dream of home ownership within their reach: increasing the term of the loan in order to reduce the monthly payments. Buyers and re-mortgagers are encouraged to tie themselves into mortgages lasting 35, 40 or even 52 years.

❝ The CCCS believes that higher mortgage payments are at the heart of very many people's debt problems. ❞

Case Study Ben Williams

Ben signed up for a mortgage with a top-ten mortgage provider and was allowed to pay back over 35 years. He couldn't afford the house he wanted or the monthly payments if he used a standard 25-year mortgage. In response, the bank said it would let him borrow more than 100 per cent of the house value and pay over a longer term. Despite not having a permanent job (he was a contract worker in the public sector), the bank allowed Ben and his partner to borrow more than four times their joint earnings. In effect, he needed to agree that he could still be 72 and paying a mortgage in order to tie up the deal. Ben felt that as the payments were the same as his rent, they posed no extra burden. That analysis, however, discounted the need to pay bills when boilers break down, gutters leak and the roof needs repair.

TAKING OUT A FIRST MORTGAGE

Most surveys that ask young people whether they would like to own their own home find the overwhelming majority say yes. Unlike continental Europe, the alternative of renting is not attractive. Britain provides tenants with few rights and allows landlords to comply with only basic standards. Millions of people, and increasingly young people, have to rent, though, because buying their own property is unaffordable.

Some banks and building societies have developed mortgages that allow homebuyers to increase the amount they can borrow, others have mortgages that extend the life of a loan. Some banks, not usually building societies, do both.

There are two main types of mortgage available to anyone buying a property: the interest-only mortgage and repayment mortgage. Then there is the off-set mortgage, which is a comparatively new product.

❝ Most young people would rather own their own home than rent. ❞

↘ The mortgage market is now so complicated it is always worth consulting a financial adviser or mortgage broker. For help finding an adviser see pages 139–42.

Interest-only mortgage

An interest-only loan only repays the interest and not the capital. The provider applies an average interest payment for the life of the mortgage and leaves you to save to pay off the capital.

Repayment mortgage

With a repayment mortgage, each monthly payment to the provider reduces a proportion of the loan and interest. In the early years, when the loan is at its largest, interest payments make up the bulk of the costs. As you begin to pay off the loan, the interest payments become smaller. At the end of the term, the loan and interest are paid in full.

The repayment mortgage is the favourite of financial advisers and consumer groups like Which?. Too many scandals in recent years involving interest-only mortgages have deterred advisers from recommending anything other than repayment mortgages (see endowments, pages 106–9).

❝An increasing number of interest-only borrowers are choosing to leave the capital sum unpaid, for a variety of reasons.❞

Off-set mortgage

Off-set mortgages have only recently become a mainstream offering. In essence, they allow you to use your savings to reduce the amount of interest you pay on your mortgage. With an off-set deal, your home loan and savings account are with the same bank or building society and kept under the same umbrella. Most people who take out an off-set mortgage keep their savings in a deposit account, separate from their mortgage.

In essence, you off-set your savings against your mortgage, so that you're only paying interest on the balance.

If you are struggling to manage your debts, then savings are probably not top of your list of priorities. And for that reason an off-set mortgage is out of the question.

Interest-only versus repayment mortgage

If you want to take out an interest-only mortgage, some providers will ask what you are doing to pay off the capital. An increasing number won't and they leave it to you to decide. A growing number of borrowers are therefore choosing to leave the capital sum unpaid. One estimate put the number of borrowers at 200,000 with interest-only mortgages who failed to set up a

 There are websites and the personal finance sections of newspapers that provide information on best buys relating to mortgages. See the box on page 100 for more information on this subject.

repayment vehicle. They are doing this for three reasons:

- **A series of scandals around mortgage savings** and investment products have deterred homeowners from adopting the same risks (see endowments on pages 106–9 for more discussion of this issue).
- **Not putting money aside** to pay for the capital sum increases a borrower's disposable income, which therefore increases the amount the borrower can spend on his or her mortgage repayment. As a result, a bigger mortgage can be applied for, which in turn allows the borrower to buy a bigger house.
- **The buyer only needs a larger home** while there are children around. After 25 years the children will have left home so the house can be sold and the capital sum repaid out of the sale proceeds, and the remainder used to buy a smaller place.

The raw figures also put the benefits of taking out an interest-only mortgage seemingly more attractive. On a repayment basis, a £150,000 mortgage fixed at 4.84 per cent costs the borrower £863 a month over the first two years. But if he or she takes an interest-only loan, the cost is just £605 a month. For a £200,000 loan, the difference is closer to £350 a month.

However, while these arguments are tempting for some families, there is the potential for them to cause terrible financial harm. Many borrowers –

particularly those who have re-mortgaged to a cheaper deal – may fail to understand that they have a loan which, when it matures in 15, 20 or 25 years' time, will leave them with a huge bill. The regulator has already begun to receive complaints in its mailbag.

An interest-only mortgage is a bet that property prices will continue to rise. Making that bet on your main residence is foolish when a fall in property prices could leave you without the money needed to pay off the capital and buy another home. Being homeless in your fifties or sixties would disastrous. Worse would be becoming homeless earlier if you were made redundant or suffered a long-term illness. A forced sale when you have only paid the interest would cut the value of your stake in the home to the

> **!** If you change your mind at a later stage and want to switch from interest-only to a repayment mortgage, the costs are high. For example, if you have a 25-year £100,000 mortgage on interest-only with another ten years to run, switching to a repayment basis increases the monthly cost from £508 to £1,115. These figures are based on a borrower paying at a variable rate of 6.1 per cent.

increase in value since you bought it. That would then leave you with only a small sum with which to buy another home.

It is therefore much safer to pay the capital and interest using a repayment mortgage and own your home outright at the end of a mortgage term.

The Financial Services Authority is concerned about the number of interest-only mortgages that are being sold. In 2006, it said: 'An analysis of data on sales of regulated mortgages between April 2005 and December 2005 indicated that an increasing number of mortgages were being completed on an interest-only basis, with the lender not recording that there was a linked repayment vehicle in place.

'Interest-only mortgages, especially ones where there is no repayment vehicle in place, may represent a greater risk to consumers than a repayment mortgage. While these are appropriate mortgages for some consumers, they are not suitable for everyone.'

❝ It is much safer to pay the capital and interest using a repayment mortgage and own your home outright at the end of the term. ❞

Getting the best deal

Even the most financially astute borrowers find themselves scratching
their heads when choosing a mortgage deal. In recent years, the
situation has become more complicated as lenders of all descriptions
have entered the mortgage market. To distinguish themselves, they
have invented all manner of novel and complicated deals.

If you are already in debt, you need to tread carefully before signing up to a mortgage loan that promises to solve all your financial problems. There are more catches and important clauses in the small print than ever before.

MORTGAGE CALCULATIONS

The maths governing mortgages can be straightforward with the simplest products. And the gains that you can make are obvious to all, which is why so many people have chosen to buy their own home.

A £150,000 home that is bought with a £20,000 deposit and £130,000 repayment mortgage will cost £250,000 in total over 25 years if the mortgage interest rate is based on today's costs of around 6.5 per cent a year. This represents an interest payment of £100,000.

Of course, while you have paid £100,000 in interest, your property has increased in value. If you expect property prices to rise on average by 5 per cent a year (double retail price inflation), then the £150,000 house will be worth £300,000 after 25 years.

This seems like a good deal to most people, which is why they say 'Yes' when asked would they become a homeowner if they had the chance. However, this plain, simple mortgage is not what most banks and building societies sell. They entice customers with deals that have become more complex with every year that passes. Signing up for a mortgage, therefore, involves some complex calculations.

Interest rates

Each mortgage deal comes with two interest rates:

- The rate for the life of the deal, e.g. two years, five years or whatever.
- The rate if you stay with that mortgage company beyond when the deal ends and pay its standard variable rate.

The advert will read something like 5.9 per cent for two years, 6.7 per cent APR. The APR figure shows the interest rate over the life of the mortgage.

93

Fees

The fees attached to the mortgage can add up to more than £1,000 and therefore need to be checked carefully. If you are re-mortgaging, there are also fees to be paid for leaving your existing provider, for which many firms are charging £300 or more as an administration fee. These are not early redemption fees (see page 99), but they are charged when you are ostensibly 'free' to leave. It is interesting how lenders have managed to squeeze this charge past the regulator (in no other industry could you be punished with a hefty charge for leaving). Nevertheless, it is popular with lenders, and is another cost that needs to be taken into account.

Adding all these fees together means that only a financial adviser or mortgage broker can tell you if it is worth paying high fees to get a low interest rate. To get you started, though, a rule of thumb is that you need a mortgage worth more than £50,000 before it is worth shopping around. You can also estimate the difference between rival mortgage deals and how much saving on the interest rate is eaten away by the cost of the fees (see the examples, opposite).

❝ Ask your adviser if it is worth paying high fees to get a low interest rate. ❞

Case Study | **Mary and Sam Seager**

Mary and Sam Seager bought their first home in June 2006. They applied for a mortgage for £190,000 through financial advisers linked to the estate agents who sold them their house. The financial advisers knew the couple already had a poor credit history. The monthly repayments were around £1,000. Shortly afterwards, Mrs Seager, a legal secretary, went on maternity leave, and Mr Seager, who was a self-employed carpenter, found work hard to find.

The high mortgage and other outstanding debts meant the couple, who were in their early thirties, soon got into difficulty with their repayments. They had a possession hearing in April 2007 and were given 28 days notice of eviction. The repayment to the mortgage company was nearly £210,000 due to the high early repayment charges.

They lost their home in only ten months and were left with charges for the repossession and penalties because of the strict conditions of the mortgage. They sought advice from a debt charity but their mortgage was so inflexible that without the income to maintain payments they had little choice but to give up their home. The mortgage company did not take into account the couple's changing circumstances or existing outstanding debts and so left them in a much worse position.

Comparing up-front costs of mortgage deals

Only a few years ago, mortgage arrangement fees and other set-up costs were pretty much the same, whichever lender you chose. Now they vary widely. Check the costs carefully because what can seem like an enticing deal can often cost you more than a simpler and more straightforward mortgage offer.

Mortgage 1: £130,000 fixed mortgage at 5.83 per cent for two years.

Fees (valuation, solicitor's fee and an arrangement fee):	£999
Divide the fee into 24 monthly payments, which must be added to the monthly mortgage instalments:	£41.62

Mortgage 2: £130,000 fixed mortgage at 6.38 per cent for two years

Fees (valuation, solicitor's fee and an arrangement fee):	waived
Therefore no fee to add to the monthly mortgage instalments	

But Mortgage 1 has a lower interest rate attached to it, so the final calculation leaves the holder of Mortgage 1 paying £865.75/month and the holder of Mortgage 2 pays £868.09/month.

So in this case, paying the fees was worthwhile.

If the fees are in excess of £1,200 on a two-year deal, then you probably need a mortgage in excess of £150,000 to make it worthwhile.

Mortgage payment protection insurance (MPPI)

MPPI provides cover if you are made redundant or have a long-term illness and are unable to find the money for monthly mortgage payments. The need for some kind of cover arises because government benefit cuts resulted in the loss of mortgage benefit. No longer were homeowners able to claim their mortgage costs when they were made redundant. Not, that is, until they have been out of work for 39 weeks, by which time most people have run out money for most things, let alone their mortgage. It works in the same way as payment protection cover (PPI) (see pages 56–8), though MPPI doesn't typically include life cover. See the table overleaf for illustrations as to the expense of an MPPI.

The potential coast of an MPPI

Compare the cost of mortgage payment protection with ten of the UK's top lenders for a 30-year-old couple with a £100,000 loan and £700 monthly mortgage repayments.

Lender	Rate per £100	Monthly cost of MPPI	Annual cost of MPPI	Total cost of MPPI over 25 years	Potential saving over one year
Abbey	£6.04	£42.28	£507.36	£12,684	£276.36
Cheltenham & Gloucester	£7.70	£53.90	£646.80	£16,170	£415.80
Woolwich	£5.95	£41.65	£499.80	£12,495	£268.80
Average	£6.14	£42.98	£515.76	£12,894	£284.76

HOW INTEREST RATES ARE CHARGED

Mortgage companies charge interest in different ways. Choosing a deal usually involves making a choice between fixing the interest you pay, a base rate tracker, a capped rate or a discount from the lender's **standard variable rate (SVR)** of interest.

Fixed rate

This should do what it says on the tin. For the length of any deal, the interest rate remains fixed at the same level. Usually, however, lenders charge a premium for giving the certainty of fixed monthly payments.

A fixed rate can last two years or anytime up to 25 years. Most people choose deals lasting two to five years. The longer the period of the deal, the more expensive they tend to be.

The cost of the mortgage is based more on predictions of future interest rates than the current interest rates. This has the effect of sometimes making them very cheap or very expensive in relation to variable rate deals.

Base rate tracker

Your mortgage is set at a figure above or below the Bank of England base. The advert might read 'Tracker mortgage at 3.5 per cent equal to Bank of England base rate 5.5 per cent minus 2 per cent'.

The gap between your interest rate and the bank base rate is maintained at all times. As a result, your monthly mortgage interest payments will go up and down in line with movements in the Bank of England base rate, tracking each twist and turn.

The main benefit of a tracker mortgage is that you quickly benefit from any cuts in rates. You will need to bear in mind, however, that base interest rates don't just go down. So when the Bank of England raises UK interest rates, the cost of your tracker mortgage will rise straightaway.

Capped rate

A capped rate operates in the same way as a discount mortgage except it can only rise to the level of the cap. This gives the customer some security that their monthly mortgage will not rise above a certain amount, but will follow rates on their way down. This facility means that at the outset you will have to accept a higher interest rate.

Discount variable rate

The interest will go up and down in line with movements in the lender's SVR. With a discount mortgage you initially pay a rate of interest that is a set amount below the lender's SVR for a specified period of time, after which you revert to the SVR.

For example, if the lender's SVR is 6 per cent and the discount is 2 per cent, the interest rate you will pay is 4 per cent. Most discounted mortgages are for two to three years, although lengthier deals are available. Many have a 'stepped discount' where the discount decreases in two or three stages.

Lenders claim this type of mortgage can cushion you from the worst of the highs and lows in the bank base rate. The lender, in effect, says it will not pass on some of the increases in rates in return for not passing on some of the cuts in rates. You get a smoothing effect and many borrowers appreciate this implicit promise.

❝ Tracker mortgages have gained in popularity as you are sure to benefit from interest rate cuts, unlike other deals. ❞

> **!** Recently, lenders have not always passed on the cuts made by the Bank of England that make your mortgage cheaper, while almost always passing on the interest rate rises. This has undermined the popularity of the discount mortgage and persuaded more people to buy tracker mortgages.

 For more information on mortgages, see the *Which? Essential Guide Buy, Sell and Move House.*

CHOOSING A MORTGAGE

Unless you have a big mortgage – and that tends to be thought of as £100,000 or more – the losses or gains from picking a particular mortgage are relatively small.

The Bank of England's stewardship of inflation has resulted in only small variations in interest rates. For instance, between the start of the decade and publication of this book, interest rates have moved within a narrow band of 3.5 to 6 per cent. It is not since the early 1990s that interest rates have hit the heights of 15 per cent.

The ups and downs of interest rates tend to even themselves out over the longer term, so what you lose today on your mortgage, you will most likely win back tomorrow. If you choose a discount mortgage or tracker, it will usually be cheaper than a fixed-rate mortgage because the lender is taking a risk agreeing to a fixed rate (the risk is that the cost of borrowing goes up dramatically and they are left out of pocket).

If you have a large mortgage, and many people in property hotspots are forced to take out huge mortgages to pay sky-high property prices, the benefits of making the right choice can be significant. There are still thousands of pounds to be saved by choosing a tracker when rates are tumbling and a fix just before they start to climb.

That said, there is still a good case for fixing your mortgage interest rate if you need to keep a close eye on your budget each month. To illustrate how much interest rate rises can dent your income,

Thinking through the costs

Let's say, when you go shopping for a mortgage, the fixed-rate offers are 1 per cent higher than the tracker/discount offers on a three-year deal. Logic says you would only buy the fixed rate if you thought interest rates were going to rise by at least 2 per cent and stay there. If the interest rate increases by 2 per cent over the next year and after a year at that rate falls back by 2 per cent, you will have roughly spent the same on mortgage repayments as if you have chosen the discount or tracker mortgage.

The gains in this example made by your discount mortgage at the beginning and end of the mortgage term are offset by losses in the middle. You might have lost by a little, but gambling with mortgage rates is no longer a sport that can save thousands of pounds for the average homeowner.

take this example:

Between the summer of 2006 and spring of 2007, rates moved up from 4.5 to 5.5 per cent. The increase meant a borrower with a typical £100,000 variable rate mortgage forked out around £64 more on monthly repayments. If it stayed that way for a year, that borrower would be forced to blow an extra £768 a year on the mortgage.

That's a large sum of money to most people and so a good reason to fix interest payments if interest rates look like they are about to start going up.

FLEXIBILITY

Mortgage products are flexible by degrees. Some are so flexible they are almost like a bank account with an overdraft. Others keep the boundaries of

"Gambling on mortgage rates can no longer save the average homeowner thousands of pounds. "

Hidden costs

Arrangement fee: Many lenders charge an arrangement fee for special deals like fixed-rate mortgages and discount mortgages. The fees have been rising rapidly in recent years. They can be a one-off payment of £500–£600 or a percentage of the mortgage. Most people add the fees to the cost of the mortgage, though this increases the total debt and increases monthly interest payments.

Banking services: Check the fees charged for transferring your mortgage and deposit money electronically. See if the transactions can be made at the same time to avoid multiple charges.

Early redemption penalties: Before choosing a mortgage, check how much you will be charged if you terminate the mortgage early. If you have signed up for a low-cost offer, whether it is a fixed rate, discount from the variable rate, capped rate or tracker, the provider will punish you financially if you quit before the contracted termination date. Worst

of the deals are the ones that lock you in to a high SVR for several years after a low offer period. In one extreme case, a lender loaned at 2 per cent for the first two years followed by its SVR of 7.8 per cent for three years. You might have wanted to switch to a better offer, but to leave the mortgage would have meant a fine worth three months of repayments at the SVR rate, making the move less attractive.

Fees charged by advisers or brokers: Anyone helping with the arrangement of your mortgage will charge for their advice. Some will just take commission from the lender; others will charge you commission. Some will do both. Make sure you look at the figures to work out if you are getting a good deal.

Higher lending charge: This is a charge you may have to pay if your deposit is less than 10 per cent. Avoid lenders who make this charge as they are usually the ones trying to make their profits on sneaky hidden charges.

 For more information on 'best buy' mortgages, go to www.which.co.uk/money.

what you can do pretty rigid. You will find that most providers allow mortgage holders to pay off at least an extra 10 per cent a year, either through higher monthly payments or using lump sums. They may also allow short repayment holidays (see page 72) should you become unemployed or have other serious financial difficulties.

Like most things in the financial services industry, if you want more of something you will need to pay for it. Extra flexibility comes at a price. Check the terms of the mortgage agreement to make sure the flexibility you want is available and not an expensive extra add-on.

Best buy tables

Online websites, the personal finance sections of newspapers (usually in the weekend editions) and consumer magazine such as *Which? Money* all have mortgage 'best buy' tables. These list the best mortgages that week or month in a series of categories. They should tell you the basic fees and charges for each mortgage product, the introductory interest rate and whether the offer is for a fixed rate, discount, tracker or other type of mortgage. If you don't feel confident figuring out which is best (for instance, whether a low rate and high fees mortgage is better for you than a no-fees mortgage with a slightly higher rate), then seek independent advice.

❝Most providers will allow mortgage holders to pay off at least an extra 10 per cent a year without a penalty.❞

Re-mortgaging

Intense competition in the mortgage market has brought a bewildering number of mortgage products to choose from, while dramatic increases in house prices have allowed a generation of homebuyers to trade in the equity in their homes either for cash to spend or to consolidate loans.

As discussed earlier, mortgage deals have become more expensive and the advantages of re-broking deals every few years less clear-cut. Nevertheless, the large amount of money involved in paying a mortgage each month means that millions of people are still doing it and making savings.

RE-MORTGAGING TO SPEND

Most people who have increased their mortgage to spend money have invested in their homes. New kitchens, bathrooms, central heating systems and extensions, with conservatories being the most popular, are often funded with increased mortgage borrowing.

Property developers joke that not all these investments increase the value of people's property, and some actually devalue them. They are the exceptions. The project is usually specific and the spending kept within sensible limits.

Even if a property developer would roll their eyes at your scheme, prices have increased so much that should you sell your home, the effect of botched jobs is disguised by rising house prices.

The cure is to take advice about the likely effect on your property's value. If you do take advice and the answer is positive, then planning to use the equity that comes from the rising value of your home is sensible. A mortgage is generally the cheapest form of debt and mainstream lenders are usually well regulated.

For a growing family stuck in a small house, a loft conversion that costs between £20,000 and £40,000 will

❝ Before re-mortgaging, take advice about the likely value of your property after you've developed it. ❞

For a list of the pros and cons of re-mortgaging, see page 185, and for more information on funding home extensions, see the *Which? Essential Guide Develop your Property*.

101

The cost of re-mortgaging

Mortgage: £200,000 mortgage to be paid over 25 years with a two-year tracker rate of 4.79 per cent, which then converts into a 6.5 per cent SVR

You would pay £1,140 a month in the first two years and £1,329 a month for the remainder of the term.

Re-mortgage: Increase the term to 40 years after the two-year deal ends

The monthly payments only increase to £1,157 – a saving of £172 a month or more than £2,000 a year. For those with tight finances, that £172 a month saving could be the difference between getting on the property ladder and being forced to continue renting.

But those lower payments come at a price. After 25 years, you would have handed over a total of £394,241 in mortgage payments, based on the above example. But with a 40-year term, the total amount repaid soars to £549,931.

Before striking a deal like this, you should be aware that the longer a mortgage runs, the older you will be when you finally pay it off.

---

generally add a similar amount to the value of their home and, more importantly, in the short term prevent them spending many times more on moving to another house.

Increasing a mortgage loan can also be a sensible way to overcome what you know will be a temporary loss of income. If one parent decides to stay at home to look after children, often because the costs of childcare make it uneconomic to work, it may be the best solution to maintain at least some of your disposable income. Extending the term of the loan can also appear sensible for the same reason (see the example, above).

 There are much higher rates of unemployment among the over fifties, a fact that increases the possibility that you will not be able to afford an expensive mortgage in later life.

66 Increasing a mortgage loan can be a good way to overcome a temporary loss of income. 99

RE-MORTGAGING TO CONSOLIDATE

If you have increased your borrowings on credit cards and loans, you may consider consolidating them within your mortgage. The benefits of this move are several:

- A mortgage is generally the cheapest form of debt.
- Mortgages are often more flexible than loans.
- Several payments to loan providers become one payment to a mortgage provider.

If it saves you money and puts your finances on an even keel, then consolidation can be part of your own

debt management plan. However, serious problems can arise when long-term mortgage borrowing is used to prop up a lifestyle that has run out of money and there is no immediate solution. Debt advisers have long lists of people who have extended their mortgages to finance non-essential items like holidays, home improvements or a new car.

Of course, you can put the loan debt on the mortgage and pay it off quickly. Some people increase their monthly payments to benefit from a combination of the cheaper mortgage rate and the shorter timescale of a loan, but that takes a good deal of discipline.

Out of the mainstream 1: sub-prime mortgages

If you have a poor credit record because you have racked up **county court judgements** for non-payment of bills or worse, bankruptcy, you will need to approach a mortgage broker for help. The broker will make an initial assessment and then contact a lender that offers so-called sub-prime mortgages if you have a badly impaired credit history. A sub-prime mortgage will have a higher interest rate as an

---

Money management tips

- The more mortgage debt you have in relation to your income, the harder it will be to get the best deals as your credit score will have declined. Mortgage companies will look unfavourably on your application for their best products. If that forces you to seek a re-mortgage at a higher rate, it will send your monthly payments up and not down.
- The solution must be to examine all outgoings to see where you can make savings. Avoid consolidating if you can help it, and if you believe there is no other option after taking advice, make it a once-in-a-lifetime experience.

Jargon buster

County court judgement A judgement for a debt by the county court. Creditors must get a county court judgement before they can instruct bailiffs to seize your possessions

insurance policy for the lender against the borrower defaulting on the loan.

There are around 25,000 mortgage advisers/brokers registered with the Financial Services Authority (FSA), which regulates mortgages. There are around 20 lenders offering sub-prime mortgages. Most of them don't credit score. They know you have a bad score. But they do check with the credit reference agencies that the defaults and other payment problems you have admitted on your application are the sum total of your financial misdeeds. There is quite a lot of paperwork, too. The lenders will want to see documents relating to your problematic past. After the credit report is analysed, they place you in a 'band', which determines how much interest you pay. This will be 3, 5, 7 or 11 per cent higher than high street lenders' standard variable rates.

As one sub-prime lender says: 'We don't reject people because they don't have a good score. We leave that to the banks and building societies. They have come to us for the very reason that they don't have a good record.'

The benefit of this type of mortgage is that you can buy a house with a mortgage when the mainstream lenders have locked you out. The mortgage can also get you back on track after a rocky time and when you may have damaged a once good credit record. The downside comes when you overstretch on a high priced loan. So you must be wary of listening to advisers, no matter how well qualified, who allow you to stretch the loan to the limit.

Out of the mainstream 2: self-certification mortgages

Self-employed people are the main target for self-certification mortgages. They may also be a viable prospect for contract workers and workers with a portfolio of different jobs.

These type of mortgages have proved popular because they allow you to get on the property ladder if you are outside mainstream full-time employment and cannot provide the usual proof of regular income demanded by lenders. You also don't need a guarantor for the loan (someone who will promise to pay if you default or run away) or an employer providing you with a letter verifying you have a regular income.

In a sense, you guarantee your own mortgage by signing a self-certification form. The lender accepts this knowing that it can repossess the property if you get into problems.

If you think this all sounds a bit easy,

Mortgage advisers/brokers can be found in the classified section of local papers or Yellow Pages. Check that the mortgage adviser/broker has the recognised qualifications - Cmap levels 1, 2 and 3. They may include their qualifications in advertising literature, otherwise you need to ask about their qualifications when you discuss the mortgage with them.

then you would be in agreement with the main financial regulator, the Financial Services Authority. The FSA has criticised financial advisers for allowing thousands of people to overstretch their finances to buy bigger homes. Many deals have unravelled and left the lender to reclaim their home.

If you are in a position to apply for a self-certification mortgage, don't exaggerate your estimated income. Taking a risk with your home is foolish when you are betting on so many things going to plan. What if your income is static or less than predicted? What if house prices decline, if only a little? You could lack the funds needed to afford monthly mortgage payments and when it is repossessed, find the home is worth less than you paid. Losing your home and repaying the negative equity to the lender could cripple your finances for years to come.

❝ Many self-certification deals have unravelled and resulted in the lender reclaiming the property from the overstretched occupier. ❞

To find an independent financial adviser, go to www.fsa.gov.uk, www.impartial.co.uk and www.find.co.uk. Always check on www.fsa.gov.uk/register to see if your adviser is authorised to offer advice.

Endowment policies

Sold mainly during the 1980s and early 1990s, endowments became a full-blown financial scandal when it was discovered that banks and insurance companies had told customers they should buy an endowment investment policy because it would pay the capital sum in their loan and probably give them a lump sum present on top.

This promise failed to materialise. Not only have endowments failed to pay lump sums to policyholders, they have fallen short of the target needed to pay the mortgage. Millions of people have found they need to spend more money topping up their mortgages to make up the shortfall.

If you haven't taken advice already about the future of your policy, then you should at the earliest possible time. Most policies are at least ten years old and time is short to make a decision about what to do next (see options on pages 108–9). There may also still be time to complain about how the policy was sold (see box, right). Millions of people have complained to the bank, building society or insurance company that sold the policy and asked for compensation. Most complaints have proved successful.

Making a complaint

Complaining to your endowment provider is relatively easy. Getting them to take responsibility for selling a dodgy product is another matter. However, it is best to start by writing a letter setting out the basics of your complaint (see the example given, opposite).

All providers have put time limits on complaints and many have declared all their customers out of time. But if you have a large policy, it could still be worth complaining. If you cannot bear the thought of a fight with the provider, there are complaints handling firms and firms of lawyers that may be interested in taking up your case for a fee. The Law Society, which regulates solicitors in England and Wales, can put you in touch with a firm that has the expertise to pursue such a case. Also seek advice from a free advice service such as Citizens Advice Bureau or the Financial Ombudsman Service (see Useful addresses on pages 212–15).

❝ Many endowments fell short of the target needed to pay off the mortgage, and millions of people had to meet the shortfall. ❞

106

Sample letter for complaining about an endowment policy

Use this template text, inserting your personal information where indicated in square brackets.

[INSERT YOUR HOME ADDRESS]
[INSERT TODAY'S DATE]

[INSERT THE NAME OF YOUR ENDOWMENT SUPPLIER]

Re: Complaint concerning advice received on endowment mortgage
[INSERT YOUR ACCOUNT NUMBER]

Dear Sir/Madam

I am writing to you to make a complaint about the way I was sold my mortgage endowment policy. I believe, for the reasons set out below, that I was mis-sold this policy and am requesting you to investigate the sale. I am also requesting that you send me a copy of my endowment file so that I can see all the documentation you have relating to my case.

An adviser in your company sold me a [INSERT THE NAME OF THE ENDOWMENT POLICY] in [INSERT MONTH AND YEAR]. The target amount was [INSERT THE AMOUNT].

The reason(s) I am complaining is/are as follows:
[USE ONE OF THESE APPROPRIATE PHRASES]

The endowment was not suitable for me.
The sale didn't follow the rules.
The endowment policy will not mature until after I retire.
I already had an endowment and the adviser told me to cash it in and sold me a new policy.
The adviser said the policy was guaranteed to pay off the mortgage.
The adviser said the policy would definitely pay off the mortgage.

I would be grateful if you could reply to this letter within 14 days and handle this complaint according to your usual complaint procedures.

Yours faithfully

[SIGN YOUR NAME]
[TYPE YOUR NAME]

Under a scheme designed by the Financial Services Authority, policies are divided into three broad categories: green, amber and red:

- Green policies are on schedule to repay the loan.
- Amber policies are off target by only a small margin.
- Red policies are failing badly.

Most policies are in the red band. If yours falls into this category, you will have received literature from the provider telling you to seek advice. You can also check documents from the provider to see if it is still going to pay off the loan.

When you see an adviser, the conversation will focus on how you plan to pay off the mortgage when your endowment policy falls short. The best plan is to find a solution now rather than allow disaster to strike in a few years.

❝ The best plan for policies in the red band is to find a solution to the shortfall now rather than allow disaster to strike in a few years.❞

OPTION 1

You could convert the portion of your home loan covered by the endowment into a repayment mortgage. This will guarantee the entire capital is paid when the term is complete, but it will increase monthly payments. These can be off-set by selling or cashing in the endowment and using the money to reduce your mortgage. You will also save on the monthly endowment policy payments.

Verdict

Safe, but leaves you paying higher monthly payments. Also, selling an endowment gives poor value for money. The cash-in values offered by insurance companies fail to reflect the endowment's true value, leaving you a loser both ways.

OPTION 2

Keep the endowment, but treat it as 'paid up'. Like Option 1 you don't put any more money in, but nor do you sell it either. This will leave a shortfall so you add to your repayment mortgage to make up the difference.

Verdict

Safe, costs more each month, but allows you to benefit from some investment growth in the endowment.

 For further information on making a complaint about an endowment policy – including more detailed reasons as to why the policy was mis-sold – go to the Which? website, which contains free expert guidance: www.which.co.uk.

OPTION 3

If your endowment was due to reach £50,000, say, but is only on schedule to pay £40,000, then you are faced with a £10,000 shortfall. You start an investment plan to bridge the gap.

Verdict

Has the risk that the endowment and the additional investment will prove to be worse than expected, leaving a still large gap in funding for the property.

OPTION 4

Do nothing. You treat the endowment as a halfway house between an interest-only loan and a repayment loan. If the shortfall is large, you sell the house and move into a smaller one.

Verdict

High risk. You are not taking control of your life. A head-in-the-sand approach allows events to dictate when you sell and when you stay. It is much better to put in place a plan that puts you in control when the mortgage term expires and the capital and interest must be paid (see options 1 to 3).

Payment difficulties

If you are experiencing difficulty meeting mortgage payments, seek advice. The worst thing you can do is delay dealing with the problem. It will only come back to bite you even harder. There are many reputable debt advice charities, including Citizens Advice (CAB) and the Consumer Credit Counselling Service (CCCS). Remember, you are not alone. Increases in interest rates since 2006 have pushed many people to the edge of bankruptcy.

❝The worst thing you can do is delay dealing with the problem, as it will only come back to bite you harder.❞

 To find your nearest CAB office go to: www.adviceguide.org.uk and for the Consumer Credit Counselling Service, go to www.cccs.co.uk.

Other options for your home

In recent years, some lenders and insurance companies have begun offering cash in exchange for a portion of your home. If you have paid off your mortgage and own your home, you can increase your income using the equity that has built over the years, but this method of raising cash is not for everybody and there are many pitfalls.

EQUITY RELEASE

There are two main types of equity release: the home reversion and the lifetime mortgage:

- **A reversion plan** allows the homeowner to sell a proportion of the home to a lender for a cash lump sum. The lender must wait until you die before it can reclaim an agreed percentage of the sale value.
- **The lifetime mortgage** operates like a mortgage except the unpaid monthly contributions accumulate or 'roll up' over the years, eating into the equity. The lender gives you a cash lump sum and then begins charging you the mortgage interest. This mounts up over time. Eventually, it can become so big that it equals the entire value of your home – but it can never exceed the value of your home.

Some people mistakenly believe that equity release plans are a painless way for all types of homeowner to raise capital from the increased value of their home. Others believe that they offer the chance of a skip-load of cash in exchange for a small slice of their home. Neither is true.

While some lenders advertise to the over fifties, it is really only the over sixties that can buy equity release plans. This is because the longer your life expectancy, the longer the lender must wait to get their money. Someone who is expected to live for another 30 years will get only a small cash payout compared to someone with 20 more years to live.

If you are 60 and predicted to live until you are 85 years old, a lender will give you a smaller cash lump sum than if you are 70 and predicted to live until you are 85 years old.

That said, almost everyone gets poor value for money and in exchange for a large slice of their home, lenders only give a relatively small amount of money.

Why then is this one of the fastest growing areas of personal finance? Desperation is the answer. For many pensioners, cashing in the value of their home, no matter how poor the deal, is the best route to a higher standard of living. Many pensioners have seen the value of their home rise by five or six times in 30 years and think they can tap it as a source of cash without troubling their children or grandchildren. However, if you are thinking of equity release, think again. Independent calculations show they are usually a bad deal. Which? has condemned equity release as the 'last resort' for pensioners.

- A reversion plan will grab nearly 60 per cent of the value of your home if you want to release 25 per cent of its value in cash at retirement.
- A lifetime mortgage may eat up the value of your home after 20 years.

For the privilege of staying in a family home long after the family has grown up and moved out, the cost is high. There is only one cheap and easy way to release value from your house and that is to sell it. Of course, this might not be an easy step to take, but it must surely be better to sell the family home than to run up debt. By releasing extra capital through selling your home, you could house your children and grandchildren at local hotels when they come to visit you. You could alternatively pass on the proceeds to your beneficiaries – but bear in mind that there are potential tax hitches with this option, so consult an independent financial adviser.

DEALING WITH RENT ARREARS

It is no wonder that so many people strive to buy their own home when the rules in the rented sector are stacked heavily in the landlord's favour. Recent changes in the law have sought to give some extra protection to tenants, in particular a rule allowing tenants to put their deposit in a separate account beyond the reach of the landlord. Yet, it is still the case that tenants' rights are few. Nevertheless, millions of people continue to rent, and not just for six months or a year, but for many years.

If you find paying the rent a struggle, you must check your budget to understand if something more fundamental is the source of the problem. If you get into rent arrears because you ignored a loss of income (maybe the loss of overtime payments), the costs of extra children or just spending too much, it can be distressing and you can end up losing your home. The law says that you are responsible for making sure your landlord gets the rent on time.

Like it or not, these rules apply whether you pay all your rent yourself or whether it's paid through housing benefit. If your council has failed to pay you housing benefit, contact your council officials to find out what has gone

For further information about releasing capital in your home, see the Which? guide to equity release (www.Which.co.uk/equityrelease) and the Essential Guide to *Giving and Inheriting*.

wrong. There could be a backlog or the council might need more information to deal with your claim.

Don't be passive. You could seek advice from your landlord or a free debt advice service (see box at foot of page). They should be able to help you make a claim. Tell your landlord what's going on and keep any correspondence.

 Just to emphasise the point, you're responsible for paying your rent, even if your tenancy agreement doesn't tell you when or where to pay it.

Money management tips

- **Sort out how much is owed in rent.** Then work out your total income, including welfare benefits.
- **If you are getting into arrears,** it can often help to contact your landlord and let him or her know you're having difficulties. If you contact your landlord by phone, always follow up with a letter, explaining again why you're having problems paying the rent. If you've lost your job or have made a benefit claim, it could be that the authorities have failed to pay the money to you.
- **If your landlord is unsympathetic,** ask for a breakdown of the rent and service charges you pay. Check the rent book and check the landlord's figures against your own records.

- **Ask if the amount of rent owing is correct.** Has your landlord recorded all your payments? You may have been asked to pay rent in advance before you moved in – if so, has this been taken into account? Have the figures been added up correctly? Are you responsible for paying all the arrears or should someone else also be paying?
- **Are you claiming all benefit entitlements?** You might have lost your job or changed jobs with a cut in income. You might have fallen ill. Other benefits you should consider claiming are council tax benefit and housing benefit to help you pay rent.

 For free debt advice, go to pages 139–42, which tell you about Citizens Advice, National Debtline, the Consumer Credit Counselling Service and Payplan among other agencies.

Tax credits

If you claim tax credits, changes in circumstances can cause havoc with the tax authority's computer. It will disregard changes in income up to £25,000 and it might not calculate correctly the amount of childcare benefit or other tax credits you are entitled to. Check the figures for the amount of money you receive to ensure as far as possible that they are correct. If in doubt, ask the tax credit helpline (0845 300 3900, open 8am-8pm) or seek free advice from the Citizens Advice Bureau, which has dealt with thousands of tax credit cases. If you get it wrong, you could be asked to repay large sums of money that could push you even further into debt. (See also the website of HMRC, which runs the tax credit system – www.hmrc.gov.uk/menus/credits.htm.)

❝ If you receive written notice of eviction, talk to a housing adviser straightaway, either at the council or a debt advice charity, which might be faster. ❞

Dealing with your landlord

This can be tricky depending on whether the landlord wants to sort things out amicably or use the debt as an excuse to evict you.

To evict you, a landlord must follow certain rules, depending on what sort of tenancy you have. Your landlord usually has to apply for an eviction order from court. However, before he or she can apply for an eviction order, the landlord should serve a special notice on you. In some cases, more than one notice is needed.

According to the Citizens Advice Bureau, if you get a written notice that your landlord wants to evict you (called a notice seeking possession), you should talk to an experienced housing adviser straightaway. Your local council will have a housing office where you can seek advice, though you will probably get a quicker response from a free debt advice charity (see pages 139–42).

When considering what to do, remember that even if you do owe rent, it is a criminal offence for your landlord to do anything that he or she knows is likely to make you leave your home. They can't harass you either. That means they can't repeatedly disturb you late at night, lock you out or disconnect supplies of water, gas or electricity.

A council or housing association tenant has even stronger safeguards. For instance, your landlord must follow several more steps before he or she can start court action to evict you.

To get money back, a landlord has little choice but to pursue court action to get a judgement that you must pay. Whether the judge will allow the eviction will depend on the kind of tenancy and the reasons for seeking eviction.

As we said before, a judge will expect you to pay rent bills and to facilitate this, the judge might give you more time to pay arrears, but he or she will think it reasonable that the landlord be paid.

The best solution must be to seek a compromise. The landlord may agree to let you pay back the money you owe in instalments. Indeed, most landlords will agree a compromise if they believe they will eventually get their money back. You do need to watch out, though, that your landlord prefers legal sanctions to a compromise deal.

 If you let the case get to court, you could lose your home and have a county court judgement against you, which can seriously restrict your ability to get credit in the future. Furthermore, a landlord who has won a county court judgement against you can make an application for money to be taken off your earnings. That or they will send bailiffs to your home to take away goods (see pages 172–5).

❝Seek a compromise, such as agreeing to pay what you owe in instalments.❞

 For more basic information on the rules regarding landlords and tenants see www.adviceguide.org.uk/index/family_parent/housing. Also, see the *Which? Essential Guide Renting and Letting.*

Getting on top of debt

This chapter is all about how to deal with your debts when things are starting to get out of control. So far you have written down a list of creditors and debts and tried to get the best deal for each one. Your credit cards, loans and mortgage should all be on the lowest interest rates your credit rating will allow.

Paying your monthly bills

Part of the problem highlighted by the previous three chapters is that switching debt around is more difficult than it was. While it's not hard to find out what are the 'best buys' from tables in newspapers and online switching websites (see page 100), they can be difficult to obtain if your credit rating is not good. They can also be expensive to set up and use.

Recently, higher interest rates have made things worse. They drive up the cost of borrowing and harm your ability to stabilise debt payments and keep them affordable. That is not to say shopping around is a futile task. It's just that it doesn't generate the same benefits as a few years ago.

❝ Many factors can knock your monthly budget plan off course. If so, start the process of negotiating with your creditors. ❞

LOOK AGAIN AT YOUR BUDGET

Your monthly budget plan may have been knocked off course after you discovered an outstanding tax bill, debts to loan companies that work door-to-door or money owed to family and friends. There might be rent arrears, a tax credit refund to pay or an unpaid utility bill, gambling debts or a large outstanding legal bill. So now it is time to get serious about your debts and begin the process of negotiating with your creditors.

If you are getting deeper into debt each month, you should look at options such as cutting back on your expenditure and generating extra income. If you have lost your job, become ill, divorced or separated from your partner, or simply overspent using loans and credit cards, you must look at your income and outgoings to see what cutbacks can be made.

 If you haven't yet made your monthly budget plan, see pages 20-5, which explain exactly how to set about this task.

MAKING CUTBACKS

If part of the problem has been a refusal to make cutbacks, then now is the time to take a fresh look at your spending. We all want to maintain our standard of living, even through hard times, and for many people it is possible to use short-term debt in order to ride out a rocky patch. **But** when your spending consistently exceeds your income it is time to sit down and take a long look at your finances and what you can do to stop things getting any worse.

To stop yourself getting depressed at the thought of going 'back to basics' you must tell yourself it is not a life sentence.

Doing without treats at the supermarket must be part of any cutbacks, as could doing without:

- A breakfast at the café or the daily cappuccino before work.
- Expensive nights out buying drinks you cannot afford.
- Supporting friends and family financially.
- Fancy holidays and big ticket items like a new flat screen telly.
- Habits like visiting upmarket clothes shops, the tanning shop or the betting office.
- If you have children, indulging them with toys and sweets and other treats like trendy clothes.

In fact, your life needs to be de-cluttered and taken back to basics until your finances are back on track.

Case Study **Robert Gibbs**

A Citizens Advice Bureau in Wales saw Robert Gibbs, 24, after he had run up unsecured debts of over £4,000 plus an unsecured loan with his bank of £15,000. When he became unemployed, he was able to negotiate reduced repayments with all his creditors except his bank who offered him a management loan to consolidate his accounts. He told them that he would not be able to afford the repayments, but the bank proceeded with the loan nevertheless. When he realised that he was unable to make any payments – his available income was nil – he went to the CAB, where he was advised to consider bankruptcy.

> ❝ If you resent having to make some cutbacks, remember this is not a life sentence. ❞

GENERATING MORE INCOME

If cutbacks only fulfil half the picture, then the other half is income. What you can do to increase your income depends on your current circumstances.

If you are unemployed

It has been true for some time that there are more vacancies in the economy than there are people out of work and claiming benefits. However, the jobs are often not in the same places as the jobless. There are also situations when taking a job that could disappear at short notice is not worth taking. The most likely outcome could be that you end up claiming benefits again with all the problems that come with that process.

If you are in work

Consider doing some overtime to boost your earnings. If overtime is not available, maybe an extra part-time job could make the difference between paying your bills and going further into debt. Part-time jobs come in many guises. It could be a weekend job in a supermarket or based on a skill you have that could be offered as a service. It doesn't need to be something complicated. Consider mowing the lawn and gardening for people in the area, window cleaning or dog walking.

Plenty of professional workers spent nights and weekends working to keep their homes from being repossessed in the recession of the early 1990s. Interest rates soared to 15 per cent and many people couldn't afford their mortgage payments. Repossessions rocketed, but so too did the number of lawyers and accountants doing two jobs to make ends meet.

Case Study **Annabelle and Robert Wray**

Annabelle and Robert Wray had several small loans with a large lender that sold loans under various brand names. They were told they could have a consolidation loan to sweep up all their debts because they were homeowners. They signed a new agreement for £20,000 unaware that this was secured on their home. The APR was 27 per cent, which meant that they would be paying back over £50,000. A debt adviser found that the secured loan agreement was most likely unenforceable because of the way the loan was set out in the agreement. But the technical issue would be hard to prove. There didn't seem to be anything that could be done about the mis-selling of the loan and the fact that the couple were unaware it was secured, because they had both signed the agreement and a charging order. As a result, Mr and Mrs Wray were at risk of losing their home, as they could no longer afford the repayments.

 If you have already tried every avenue to find work and been unsuccessful, then see pages 120-3 to make sure you are getting the maximum state benefits.

If you have a spare room

The government recently relaxed the tax rules on letting a room, making it tax free up to a maximum income of £4,250. That means you can earn an extra £81.73 a week from lettings before paying tax. Families may find this solution difficult, though it has been known for children to squeeze into a couple of rooms while a third room is rented out to make ends meet.

Your lodger can occupy a single room or an entire floor. However, the scheme does not apply if your home is converted into separate flats that you rent out. In this case, you will need to declare your rental income to HMRC and pay tax in the normal way. Nor does the scheme apply if you let unfurnished accommodation in your home.

Single people living in a two-bedroomed flat can more easily make some extra money by sharing. If you are paying a mortgage, then you will need to inform the mortgage lender. If you are a tenant, then you must check the rules in your agreement on sub-letting.

Unwanted possessions

Another source of income is unwanted possessions that can be sold to generate cash. Probably the most popular method is using eBay (www.eBay.co.uk), the online marketplace. Millions of people buy and sell anything from bicycle wheels to cars on the site. Antiques and bric-a-brac are also popular. You could set yourself up with an account and attempt to offload items you don't need anymore. Alternatively, you can use Loot (www.loot.com), which is a newspaper and a website advertising what other people have to sell. Both eBay and Loot charge sellers a fee to display goods on their sites.

Car boot sales take place all over the country and are another route to selling unwanted belongings from your house, or even wanted belongings that you don't think you can afford anymore. You will pay a fee to sell at a car boot sale. The fee varies and depends on the area and how big the venue is and how many buyers usually show up. The only rules are the usual ones about only using

❝ A spare room could be a welcome source of extra income. ❞

 Only one note of caution, be careful about the tax you might need to pay on trading profits. For more guidance see the *Which? Essential Guide Tax Handbook*.

 There are websites that tell you about local car boot sales, including www.carbootjunction.com.

descriptions that fit the goods you are selling. So if something doesn't work that you say does work, the buyer can seek you out and take you to the small claims court if you refuse to reimburse them. Obviously this only happens when the goods on sale are of a high value.

ARE YOU ELIGIBLE TO CLAIM BENEFIT?

Many of the people who get into financial difficulties are on low incomes. Research has consistently shown that significant numbers of people on the lowest incomes do not claim their full entitlement to benefits.

It's easy to see how people fail to take up benefits. The process can seem daunting, however there are experts on the end of a helpline to take you through it. Staff on government-run helplines are supposed to know the full range of benefits and support you in making a claim (see box, below).

Tax credits

Around nine in every ten families are eligible for tax credits. They can pay substantial amounts of money each month for you and your family:

- **If you are out of work** and can only find low paid employment, tax credits will supplement your income to make work pay.

- **If you lose your job,** tax credits can bridge a temporary period of unemployment.
- **If you are sick or disabled** while in work, tax credits can replace lost income.
- **If you are in employment,** whether short-term contract work/temporary jobs or long-term full-time employment, tax credits can top up your earnings.

Tax credits can pay for much of your childcare bills to help both parents stay in employment. More than £2 billion of tax credits go unclaimed each year and you might be eligible but not claiming or under claiming, based on your current income. On the otherhand, more than £6 billion was overpaid to claimants in its first three years, much of which tax credit officials have clawed back, often causing great hardship to families denied part of their income. You don't want this to happen to you if you can help it. You therefore need to check you are in receipt of tax credits and that the amount you receive is correct (see box, opposite).

Most tax and benefits experts would admit this isn't easy as the tax credit system is notoriously complex and has bamboozled some of the country's brightest brains. It has been plagued by errors and fraud since it started in

 For advice on claiming benefit, visit Jobcentre Plus. To find your nearest centre, go to www.jobcentreplus.gov.uk or call 0800 055 6688.

How the tax credit system works

To claim, phone the tax credit helpline on 0845 300 3900, 8am-8pm. The entire application can be made over the phone and the office sends you a form to confirm the details afterwards.

- Payments are based on your prediction of yearly income. The tax credit office uses your last year's income as a basis for the calculation, unless you say otherwise. If you know your earnings will drop in the coming year, you could be eligible for more tax credits.
- After the tax credit office agrees a payment, you only need to inform them once a year of changes to your income, unless it has increased by more than £25,000 (which can happen when one partner goes back to work).

You also need to inform HMRC if childcare costs go up or down (for instance, if you take up extra days at a nursery) within a month of the change happening.

The maximum amount of childcare that can be taken into account is £175 per week for one child, and £300 per week for two or more children. Only 80 per cent of childcare costs can be met. This means that the most that can actually be included towards childcare costs is £140 per week (80 per cent of £175) for one child and £240 per week (80 per cent of £300) for two or more children.

If you have two children, your tax credit payments can add up to more than £5,000 a year, depending on your income. This is a substantial amount of money, which is why, despite the potential difficulties of obtaining it, you need to check the figure to make sure you are receiving the right amount.

2003. The computer that handles the tax credit payments often makes mistakes, though more frequently errors result from inputting mistakes by tax credit staff who, it is widely acknowledged, have a creaking system to work with.

❝ More than £2 billion of tax credits go unclaimed each year and you might be eligible for them. ❞

To find out more about tax credits, go to www.hmrc.gov.uk and click on the 'tax credit' link in the 'Individuals and employees' box on the home page. Alternatively contact the HM Revenue & Customs (HMRC) tax credit office on 0845 300 3900.

If you are unemployed

If you are unemployed, the first point of contact is the local Jobcentre Plus (see box, below). If you are eligible for any benefits, including tax credits, staff at the office should be able to explain how to make a claim. They will also be able to source grants and one-off payments to support your efforts to get back into work, though these usually apply to the longer-term unemployed.

As with tax credits, there has been plenty of criticism of Jobcentre Plus and the way it dispenses advice. The government has continually reorganised the service and staff unions claim the constant turmoil leads to low morale and a poor service for its customers. That said, you will need to visit your local Jobcentre Plus for all your benefits advice if you claim Income Support or Jobseeker's Allowance. If you don't claim these benefits, you can get information about housing benefit and council tax benefit from your local council-run benefit office (phone your town hall for details).

If you have a mortgage

If you have paid for a mortgage payment protection policy as part of your mortgage (see page 95), you need to check the policy is current and telephone your mortgage company and ask for a claim form to cover monthly mortgage payments. Policies usually pay out for a year. If you don't have any cover for mortgage payments, you must contact your mortgage provider and talk to them about your situation. If your provider is unsympathetic and demands you continue to pay the agreed monthly repayments, seek advice from a free debt adviser.

Government help towards mortgage payments is available for some homeowners depending on their circumstances. This benefit, known as Income Support for Mortgage Interest (ISMI), is not paid immediately, mainly because the government wants us all to take out private insurance. If you qualify, you will not see a penny until nine months after you become unemployed (earlier assistance may be available if you took out the mortgage before 2 October 1995). This means that when payment does begin your arrears could already be substantial. Again, you must talk to your lender about how to go about paying off arrears.

You will not qualify for government help if you have a joint mortgage and only one of you loses your income – even if your partner works as little as 16 hours a week. Nor will you qualify if

To find your local Jobcentre Plus and to see what else it can do for you, go to www.jobcentreplus.gov.uk. If you want to make a claim for benefit, telephone 0800 055 6688 (8am-6pm Monday to Friday).

you have savings of more than £8,000. Furthermore, if you do qualify, it will only cover the interest payments on the first £100,000 of your mortgage – capital repayments, investment premiums and insurance premiums are not included.

If you have divorced or separated

When there are children involved, contact the Child Support Agency (CSA) if you haven't done so already (see box, below). This offshoot from the Department of Work and Pensions has the task of working out how much each parent should commit in financial terms towards bringing up their children. The CSA uses information given to the agency by both parents to decide if one of the parents is eligible to pay child maintenance and to work out the amount that should be paid.

The agency will ask the non-resident parent's employer or HMRC about how much they earn. It calculates child maintenance by applying one of four rate bands to the non-resident parent's income. Income is earnings, pensions and tax credits. The amount of income left after things like income tax, National Insurance and any money paid into a pension scheme have been taken off is used to make the calculation.

Jargon buster

Housing Benefit If you rent accommodation from a private landlord, you can receive an allowance paid to you by your local council to help you with your rent. Also called rent allowance

Income Support A benefit that provides financial help for people between 16 and 60 who are on a low income and not in full-time paid work and not claiming other benefits. It is not paid to unemployed people actively seeking work (they can claim Jobseeker's Allowance)

Income Support for Mortgage Interest (ISMI) This benefit is paid to homeowners who are made redundant, unemployed or ill, but only after nine months

Jobcentre Plus The government-run chain of offices that deal with job hunting and benefit claims. For information about your local branch, visit the Department of Work and Pensions' website: www.dwp.gov.uk

Jobseeker's Allowance For people who are available for and actively seeking work. To apply, visit a Jobcentre Plus office. They might make you claim with your partner

To discover how the four bands could affect your income, check the Child Support Agency's website (www.csa.gov.uk) or phone 08457 133 133. Lines are open 8am-8pm (Monday-Friday) and 9am-5pm (Saturday). The *Which? Essential Guide Divorce and Splitting Up* also gives more information on this subject.

Priority lenders

Now that you have drawn up your debt repayment or management plan and know just how much money you can offer your creditors, you are in a position to start negotiations. Start with the priority lenders and then move to the non-priority lenders, who are covered on pages 129–31.

MORTGAGE ARREARS

You don't want to lose your home, so as soon as you have difficulty paying a mortgage, you should contact your lender. Talk to them about your difficulties. You can negotiate reduced mortgage payments for a period of time or a moratorium on payments (the same as a payment holiday), which can give some breathing space while you get yourself sorted out.

Most lenders belong to trade bodies with codes of conduct. The codes spell out how they must be sympathetic to cases of genuine hardship and offer support where possible. However, a lender will usually only allow reduced payments or a payment holiday for a few months before it demands you agree on a longer-term strategy.

If you know your situation is unlikely to change in the near future, it may be

 If you fall into arrears, you might incur penalty charges, which vary depending on the lender. Check there are no charges and that you can clear the arrears and debt within the remaining period of the mortgage.

better to consider re-mortgaging with a longer term (see page 102) or selling the property and moving to one that is cheaper to buy and cheaper to run.

SECURED LOAN ARREARS

A secured loan (see pages 71–2), is like a second mortgage on your property. In that sense it should be treated in the same way as your first mortgage. The

 See the table on pages 18-19 for a description of the main divisions of priority and non-priority debts.

main difference, however, is the type of company that you will encounter when taking out a secured loan. Secured loan companies tend to be more aggressive in their stance towards customers when things start to go wrong.

If your main mortgage is taken out with a building society or bank you will probably find them more understanding than the loan company that enticed you to take out a secured loan, most likely to consolidate other debts. This is not universally true. There are tough high street banks and loan companies that will be understanding, but you should make sure you contact the secured loan company to explain the situation at the earliest possible moment.

RENT ARREARS

If you are on a low income, you might be eligible for Housing Benefit. Contact your local council to make a claim or, if you are in receipt of Jobseeker's Allowance, contact your local Jobcentre Plus for more information.

It can take several months to arrive in your bank account, depending on the efficiency of the council where you make a claim, but it can cover rent payments, or at least a large slice of them.

However, even a successful claim will leave you with arrears, so make an offer to your landlord to pay them. Suggest making small additional payments each month. Before you do this, check your tenancy to ascertain how secure you are. The landlord might cause trouble and try to evict you once you confirm you have financial problems. He or she should agree to small payments each month to repay arrears. A social landlord, like a housing association, or the council itself should be sympathetic. Check, too, with a local housing adviser if necessary – councils often have neighbourhood advice centres for housing queries – or your Citizens Advice Bureau.

COUNCIL TAX ARREARS

With soaring council tax rates in recent years it is no surprise that levels of arrears have increased as well. Unfortunately, almost two million people eligible for council tax benefit fail to make a claim each year. Most of them are pensioners, who are one of the groups with the fastest growing levels of debt.

To claim council tax benefit, contact your town hall and ask for a claim form. Most councils will also have information on their website. If you are in arrears, councils can send round the bailiffs if you don't clear the debt within a year. Some stick to the rules, others are more conciliatory (or incompetent) and allow longer repayment periods.

If you show council staff your debt repayment plan and correspondence with other creditors, they should allow you more leeway to make good arrears. But if they are unsympathetic, they can apply to the court for full repayment and ask the Department of Work and Pensions to make deductions from any benefit you receive. The council can also employ bailiffs to seize your belongings and use 'reasonable force' to get into your home. As a last resort, the council can try to persuade a magistrate that you are guilty of 'wilful refusal' or 'culpable neglect'. If found guilty, you can be sent to prison.

Of course, these actions are at the extreme end of the spectrum and, as long as you can show that you are in genuine financial trouble, are unlikely to happen to you.

GAS/ELECTRICITY ARREARS

Your gas and electricity suppliers are under a duty of care to customers and should not rush to cut supplies except as a last resort. However, they can cut supplies for non-payment of bills.

If you have a direct debit with a fuel supplier, they will probably seek to increase your monthly payments to bring down arrears. If this makes your general situation worse, contact the supplier and explain the situation. They will often allow periods of up to two years to pay off debts.

INCOME TAX OR VAT ARREARS

HM Revenue & Customs (HMRC) has more power than any other institution to pursue you for arrears. If you are self-employed and spent your tax money to keep yourself afloat, it is important to contact HMRC before it starts levying fines, surcharges and interest to your tax debt.

If you cannot afford an accountant, you can contact a tax enquiry centre, which is the new name for local tax offices. These are run by HMRC (see box, opposite) and the staff are supposed to be helpful, although there is no charter or bill of rights for taxpayers to protect you from unsympathetic staff.

If you are on a low income, you can contact the charity TaxAid for advice (see also box, opposite).

If you are registered for VAT and have failed to pass it on to HMRC, you must get in touch to arrange a repayment programme. You should take advice from an accountant or qualified tax adviser if this is the case. If your income has fallen below the VAT threshold of £64,000 turnover, you should de-register.

Money management tip

If you are concerned about your ongoing spending, you could switch to a pre-paid meter. You pay for the fuel using a key (electricity) or smartcard (gas). Until a few years ago these methods of payment were on a higher tariff and, in effect, punished people on low incomes. Most suppliers now charge the same rate for pre-pay meters as standard.

If you fail to pay either income tax or VAT, then HMRC can come after you through the courts. Depending on your situation (debts of less than £2,000), it may apply to the magistrates court for a repayment order or to instruct bailiffs and a warrant to break into your property.

If your arrears are persistent and you have failed to convince tax officials that you are willing and able to repay, HMRC can apply for a bankruptcy order. Like other creditors, it can push you towards bankruptcy if your debts exceed £750 (see page 157).

MAGISTRATE COURT FINES

Hundreds of complaints each year are sent to the TV Licensing Authority for the way it moves with lightning speed to punish people who fail to pay their TV licence. Failure to keep up instalments can result in an appearance at the local magistrates court along with people who have failed to pay National Insurance contributions and countless other criminal offences. Fines may be set at an initial hearing or automatically as the result of a fixed penalty notice.

Fines are a priority debt because the magistrates court has the power to send you to prison for non payment. It is important to ensure that the court has information about your personal circumstances because this may affect how much you are ordered to pay and whether or not you can pay off the fine in instalments.

The court can also employ bailiffs if it believes they would prove effective in retrieving the debt by confiscating your belongings. (See pages 167–78 for more on bailiffs)

If you can't afford to pay the fines, write to the fines office at the court that holds the fine. Explain your situation and, if you can, make an offer of repayment. Write a personal budget stating your income and outgoings and send a copy to the court. You may then be asked to attend a court hearing, although if they have clear information about your circumstances, they may accept your repayment offer without calling you in again.

> **❝HMRC can apply for a bankruptcy order if your arrears are persistent and they are not convinced you are willing and able to repay.❞**

 To find your local tax enquiry centre look up 'Inland Revenue' in the phone book or go to www.hmrc.gov.uk. For TaxAid, their website is www.taxaid.org.uk or telephone their helpline on 020 7803 4959, 10am-12 noon (Monday-Thursday).

CHILD SUPPORT ARREARS

Many parents who have split from their partners complain that they pay too much child support. Whatever the rights and wrongs of that argument, if you are the non-resident partner and your income has fallen, you can notify the Child Support Agency (CSA) to be reassessed. A reassessment can also take place if you have fallen into arrears and are struggling to pay bills.

If you have fallen into arrears, you need to find a way to make repayments. If a maintenance order was imposed by a court, you will need to go back to there for a new hearing. Depending on your circumstances, a 'means enquiry hearing' can order that the arrears are written off (remitted) or clawed back slowly using a direct debit payment.

But the court can also decide you must pay in full. And like other priority lenders, you must come to some arrangement or they can take drastic action. In this instance, the CSA can:

- Authorise your employer to make deductions from your wages, or
- Apply to the magistrates court for a liability order.

These are both extremely serious. A loss of wages will hamper your ability to deal with other debts. A liability order can either lead to the CSA using bailiffs or putting a charge on your house or seizing money direct from your bank account. If you get to the point where a court is about to impose these measures on you, contact your local Citizens Advice Bureau.

“The Child Support Agency can take drastic action if you fall into arrears with your payments. ”

To find your local Citizens Advice Bureau (CAB), go to www.adviceguide.org.uk.

Non-priority lenders

While priority lenders can take away your home or put you in prison for non-payment of debts, non-priority lenders shouldn't be discounted. They can still take you to court and attempt to seize your belongings. But your home is safe and they certainly can't send you to prison.

NON-PRIORITY LENDERS ARE IMPORTANT

They are probably the first creditors you will call and if you successfully make a settlement with them, you may need never trouble the priority lenders who can cause so much damage. Non-priority debts include:

- **Credit debts,** such as overdrafts, unsecured loans, hire purchase, store cards, credit cards and catalogues.
- **Student loans.**
- **Benefits overpayments.**
- **Money borrowed** from friends or family.

Start the process by contacting the creditors as early as possible by writing them a letter. It is tempting to phone using the telephone numbers on statements, but call centres are notoriously bad at maintaining a record of conversations over a period of weeks or months. A letter, however, can be duplicated several times and sent to different lenders. You can also keep a dated copy for your records.

Call your lenders as well if you believe you are about to incur heavy penalties, fines, surcharges or higher interest payments. Ask to speak to someone senior who may have more authority to agree a deal.

If you are successful in stopping further costs, write down the name of the person you dealt with and the date and time. Then repeat in a letter the agreement you reached and send it to the lender, just to make sure it is honoured.

Money management tips

- **Alert creditors early and explain why you are in debt.**
- **Work out your income and expenditure so you know how much spare money there is to pay debts.**
- **Don't borrow money to repay your debts.**
- **Don't be bullied into favouring one creditor more than others. Treat creditors fairly.**
- **Don't be bullied into paying more than you can afford.**
- **Always reply to letters from creditors, especially court letters.**

Dealing with an aggressive lender

If one or more of your creditors refuses to agree a deal, stick to your guns. If you agree to hand over more money each month to one creditor, it might keep an aggressive lender at bay, but the rest of your finances will suffer and you may not be able to make other repayments.

A lender might try to sell you a consolidation loan as a route out of your troubles (see page 73). Resist the temptation. Take advice from a debt charity. Another loan will usually mean increasing the size of the debt overall and the length of time taken to pay off the loan. Neither should be considered if you cannot pay. In this situation, the lender needs to write off some arrears and not roll them up into another expensive loan.

❝ If one of your creditors refuses to agree a deal, remain firm. ❞

If a debt collection agency becomes involved

There is a good chance that if you miss several payments, a lender will sell your debt to a debt collection agency. These agencies often buy debt very cheaply from mainstream lenders. By this we mean the agencies will pay 5–10 per cent of the value of the debt to the lender. It will then take on the responsibility of recouping the losses. If it gets an average of 15–20 per cent back from you, it has doubled its money.

So while a debt collection agency has the reputation of being scary and aggressive in the way it extracts cash from debtors, it is very likely to accept less payment than the mainstream lender, which might have rejected offers below 50 per cent of the debt.

Once you hear from the agency you need to act quickly. The aggressive side to its activities centres on its use of penalty charges to drive up the debt

---

Case Study **June Allen**

June Allen's only income is the state pension and the means tested top-up benefit, pension credit, yet she had over £80,000 of debt on both credit cards and bank loans. The debt was made up of 15 credit and store cards and seven bank loans/overdrafts.

Birmingham resident Ms Allen overspent when she retired in order to maintain her standard of living. Then she began to pay old debts with new

borrowings. The 72-year-old had no means of paying back more than £1 per month to any of her 15 creditors.

Some creditors sent her letters asking her to increase payments to £5 per month. Each time the letters arrived, she took them to her local Citizens Advice Bureau for an adviser to call the creditor and explain she couldn't pay more than she was doing already.

and force you into paying the bill. By sending the agency your original letter and financial statement listing your income and expenditure (you could send lenders a copy of the budget plan you constructed in chapter 1), you can stop these charges in their tracks.

Ignore the debt collection agency and the problem can escalate quickly. It may issue a **summons** (take out a claim) against you. This will be followed by a **default notice**, which is the stage before a full county court hearing. The letter will contain an **admission form**, which is your opportunity to pay and avoid the court.

Your offer of payment should be in line with your repayment plan and on a pro-rata basis with other lenders. Pro-rata means that each creditor gets repaid according to the size of the debt you have with them. Just because one has taken you to court does not mean you can give it special treatment. If these

Jargon buster

Default notice A form sent by creditors, but this is a legal procedure to protect lenders and not something to worry about. The default notice must allow you at least seven days to comply with the action required. It doesn't necessarily mean the creditor intends to take you to court, especially if you pay the bill

Summons A call to attend a court hearing

tactics fail, you will definitely need expert help (see pages 139–42).

> **《《**Once you hear from a debt collectiion agency, act quickly to avoid penalty charges.**》》**

Key steps to dealing with a debt collection agency

- Lender sells your debt to a debt collection agency.
- The debt collection agency writes to you demanding payment.
- You write to the agency with a financial statement.
- Agency agrees to your plan and you can start paying off your debt.

BUT, if you ignore the payment demand or the collection agency wants payment in full:

- A summons will arrive.
- Followed by a default notice to attend a court hearing (county court).
- You can avoid this by filling in the enclosed repayment form and start paying off the debt.
- If you have no money to pay the debt, you must attend the hearing and persuade the judge that your repayment plan is reasonable.

Making plans

No one wants to end up in court. It is possible to negotiate with your creditors and strike a deal early on, but as we have seen, they can object and even get aggressive. To avoid this situation developing, you can propose a more formal arrangement with the help of a free debt adviser. This will take the heat out of the situation and creates a buffer, in the shape of the debt adviser, between you and your creditors.

If you haven't already drawn up a debt plan for all your creditors, you will definitely need to do it now. It is important to take another close look at your finances and decide what sort of debt plan you will follow. There are two types of debt repayment plan:

- **The first is an informal arrangement** with your creditors. It is arranged by an adviser but still leaves you to manage the repayments following an agreement.
- **The second is a formal arrangement** that puts debt repayments in the hands of some debt charities or a debt management firm. A fee is charged that is taken out of your debt repayments.

A DEBT REPAYMENT PLAN

This option is cheaper than a debt management plan and puts you in charge of repayments, although you don't have to deal with creditors yourself as that job can be passed to a debt advice charity, such as the Citizens Advice Bureau or

National Debtline (see pages 139–40). And as luck would have it, the government has dramatically increased its funding for charities that offer advice to people who are in debt.

Take the following steps:

1 Work out how much 'spare' money you have each month (see the money management tips, page 134).
2 Make a monthly budget plan showing your income and outgoings (see pages 120–5).
3 Own up to your creditors about your situation. Do this with a letter to each lender (see the example given opposite). In your letter, tell the lenders about how you plan to pay off the debt:
   – If you have a job, tell them about your role and your prospects if they are positive.
   – If you are unemployed and searching for work, emphasise what you are doing to find a job.
4 Send off the letter together with a copy of your budget plan.

Sample letter to a creditor

If you are making no offer or token payments only, you can write out this example letter and send it to your creditors with a copy of your personal budget. Choose the points that fit your circumstances and make any other changes you need to explain your situation to your creditors.

[INSERT THE NAME OF YOUR CREDITOR]   [INSERT YOUR ADDRESS]
[INSERT THE ADDRESS OF YOUR CREDITOR]

[INSERT DOAY'S DATE]

Re: Account number [INSERT YOUR ACCOUNT NUMBER]

Dear Sir/Madam

Since making the above agreement with you, my circumstances have changed. I cannot now afford the agreed monthly payments because ... [Explain here what the problems are, such as you have lost your job, separated from your partner or had an unexpected increase in outgoings or a drop in income].

I enclose a personal budget sheet that shows my total income and the total outgoings of my household. As you can see, I have no money left to make offers of payment to my creditors.

Because of my circumstances, please agree that I can suspend payment for six months/make a token offer of £1 a month for the next six months [Decide if you are making a token offer of payment or asking the creditors to accept no offer of payment and delete as necessary].

If my circumstances improve, I will contact you again [See also the advice in step 3, opposite; anything positive you can tell your creditor about your prospects is helpful].

Please send a paying-in book/standing order form [Only include this if you are offering a token payment. Choose the payment method you want].

Thank you for your help. I look forward to hearing from you as soon as possible.

Yours faithfully

[SIGN YOUR NAME]
[TYPE YOUR NAME]

Lenders will make up their own minds about how much you should repay based on your budget. But their claim on your finances is only an opening gambit in a negotiation. As the negotiations proceed, remember that you are the one who really knows what you can afford, not them.

A debt advice charity will offer you help at every stage of your negotiations with creditors.

The main problem arises when your best efforts are rejected by lenders. For a debt repayment plan to work, you need all of them to agree. If one lender refuses to accept your offer, then it can continue to obtain county court judgements (see pages 168–9). It can also use bailiffs and court orders to obtain its funds, or ultimately apply for a bankruptcy order against you (see pages 157–60).

The problem may centre on trust. If you have missed several payments in the past, your lenders may refuse to believe that you will keep up a regular pattern each month without a concrete payment plan in place.

Money management tips

- **Tell lenders they must stop all interest and charges** accumulating on your debt. It is most likely that punishing penalty charges and extra interest payments are already a key feature of your debt and you don't want any more added to the total.
- **Don't be bulldozed into paying more than you can afford.** Look again at your monthly budget plan on pages 22-5. Make sure you have accounted for all your spending. If there are any financial problems lurking in the not too distant future that can knock you off course, include them in the budget.
- **Don't make debt repayments a life sentence.** After you have worked out what your maximum monthly payments will be, set a five-year time limit: 60 monthly payments. If you are able to pay £120 a month, you will repay £7,200 during that time. If your current total debt is £14,400, then you will be offering to repay half your debt.
- **Spread your debt repayments evenly among lenders.** Some lenders will scream louder than others or be less inclined to accept an offer. If you show them all the calculations and that you are promising to repay the same amount as other lenders, they should agree.
- **If you don't feel able to call lenders yourself** and negotiate (see pages 132-5, then you can approach one of the debt charities like Citizens Advice, the CCCS or National Debtline. They will undergo the same process on your behalf.

How to pay each creditor

The Citizens Advice Bureau gives this example:

You have total debts of £15,000. You have available income of £200 a month. You owe £10,000 to credit card company A and £5,000 to credit card company B.

Credit company A

Multiply £10,000 (debt to company A) by £200 (your available income). This equals £2,000,000.

Divide this by £15,000 (your total debt). This gives you the sum of £133 per month to offer to company A.

Credit company B

Multiply £5,000 (debt to company B) by £200 (your available income). This equals £1,000,000.

Divide this by £15,000 (your total debt). This gives you the sum of £66 per month to offer company B.

The courts use this system for working out what you can reasonably afford to pay and it is accepted by most creditors.

Key steps if your attempts to negotiate by yourself have failed

- Debt repayment plan refused
- Lender applies for county court judgement (see pages 168-9)
- Debtor requests debt management plan (DMP)
- One lender refuses, DMP not possible
- Lender obtains county court judgement, sends bailiffs (see pages 172-5)
- Debtor refuses access
- Lender applies for a bankruptcy order against you (see pages 157-60)
- Debt adviser presents new DMP
- Majority of lenders agree to DMP
- Bankruptcy avoided

A DEBT MANAGEMENT PLAN (DMP)

A typical DMP consolidates all of your unsecured debts into a single and more affordable monthly repayment, which is then paid to creditors on a pro-rata basis over an agreed period of time. A debt adviser will take on the role of handling your debts. If you choose a private company to manage your repayment plan, make sure you use one that is fully licensed and adheres to the DTI's debt management guidelines. Check with the Office of Fair Trading that the company holds a licence and has not breached the guidelines in the past.

The adviser will also enter into direct negotiations with your creditors to organise the repayment of the debts. The Consumer Credit Counselling Service (CCCS) (see page 141), for instance, handles thousands of debt management plans each year, although debt management companies will also set up a DMP (but see pages 130–1).

❝ The flexibility of a DMP allows lenders to raise the payments. ❞

Continuing to reduce your debt

It is in your own interests to maintain the payments because failure to pay could result in creditors cancelling the agreement and demanding repayment of their debts in full. This situation should be avoided at all costs. If you start to have problems making payments, contact the administrator who can re-negotiate the deal.

As you can see, the flexibility that is part of a DMP cuts both ways. A debt management company keen on you signing up for an expensive legal contract will warn that a DMP, just like an informal repayment plan, allows lenders to increase the monthly payments if they wish and so you would be better off with an individual voluntary agreement (IVA), where this can't happen. In fact, each DMP should be regularly reviewed with the aim of exploring whether you can settle with creditors earlier than first thought. But it also allows you to tell creditors when there are problems and negotiate a lower monthly payment, which you can't do with an IVA.

(See pages 147–50 for a description of an IVA together with its pros and cons and when you might choose one over a DMP.)

 The website for the Office of Fair Trading is www.oft.gov.uk or telephone their helpline on 08457 22 44 99.

Creating a debt management plan

Review your budget

As with all debt advice, the process starts with a detailed review of your household budget to determine a realistic, affordable monthly amount that can be paid to creditors, taking into account essential outgoings, such as the mortgage or rent.

Determine how much 'spare' money you have

The plan should ensure that you won't get any further into arrears or miss paying any of your priority commitments, such as your mortgage or rent, car finance, utility bills and council tax (see pages 20–5).

Your adviser contacts your creditors

Once you have agreed to the plan, your adviser will contact your creditors and present them with a detailed statement of your financial affairs. Then the adviser will offer a monthly payment based on the finances available, usually a stated number of pence for every £1 of debt.

Your adviser asks for interest to be frozen

The adviser will ask creditors to freeze interest and other charges, such as penalty fees. Creditors will also be asked not to take any legal or any other action to recover the debt, providing the debtor keeps to the terms set out in their DMP.

Your adviser negotiates your repayment fee

The adviser should also use all their experience to negotiate a full and final settlement at the lowest possible level and cut your debt payments.

Your adviser writes to your creditors to confirm the plan

Unlike an informal agreement, to which all creditors must agree, a DMP needs only 75 per cent agreement of creditors to be binding on the rest. Letters are sent to the creditors and they should agree the plan.

You pay a monthly fee to your advice charity/company

Once the plan is in place, you pay a monthly fee to the debt advice charity or management company handling your plan. The adviser passes the funds to the creditors on a pro-rata basis until the successful completion of the plan.

You pay an administration fee

In addition to paying off your debts, you will pay a fee to the administrator of the plan equivalent to 15–17 per cent of the debt you have agreed to repay. Include this figure in your calculations. So if your debts are £20,000, you divide this figure by 100 and then multiply it by 17 – £3,400 would be the administration fee.

Once a DMP is completed, you will be considered debt free and be able to make a fresh financial start. Your credit rating will have suffered some damage, but not as much as if you opted for bankruptcy or an IVA.

Money management tips

- Establish any charges that you will have to pay for an administrator's services.
- Remember, when a debt adviser works for a not-for-profit organisation it only means they don't have shareholders. They could still be a disreputable business selling DMPs and IVAs when clients could benefit from an informal arrangement.
- Make sure the proposed monthly payments are affordable.
- Ask to see evidence that they are trying to or have secured a freeze on all charges and interest and ensure that this continues during the DMP.
- Cancel direct debits to your creditors to avoid the possibility of them being paid twice.
- You can sign a DMP whether you are a tenant or homeowner or if you are living with your parents.
- If you have a partner, tell him or her about your problems. It always pays to be honest.
- While creditors don't need to agree a DMP, they must, by law, accept all offers of payment you make to them.

Getting free expert help

Why pay when you can get advice for free? Some people think the advice they pay for will be more sophisticated or the advisers working for private (profit-making) companies will be more aggressive with their creditors and drive a harder bargain on repayments, making sure they are lower. That is certainly what the new breed of debt management companies say in their daytime TV adverts.

However, the free services mentioned below have a long history of helping people from all walks of life with their debt problems. They are more independent and will be working with the same information about your finances as a private firm. If you don't have any money, you cannot make large repayments to your creditors. That is not to say all private sector firms are expensive and lack independence, but deciding which is OK and which isn't is too difficult.

CITIZENS ADVICE BUREAU

The Citizens Advice Bureau (CAB) is a charity and is the country's largest single provider of free, confidential and independent debt advice. It is undergoing a huge expansion in the number of trained advisers at its bureaux following a large injection of cash from the government. Only a few years ago, CAB suffered complaints in some parts of the UK that waiting times to see an adviser were too long, but hopefully that is no longer the case. More than half of all cases seen by CAB concern debt. A few facts about the charity:

- **It has 2,000 bureaux** across England, Wales, Scotland and Northern Ireland.
- **It is funded by grants** from the Department of Trade & Industry, local authorities and private donations.
- **You can find** your nearest bureau in the local telephone directory or by looking on their website: www.adviceguide.org.uk. The website also has a comprehensive set of guides for managing debt.

The nature of the organisation is that it gives advice about almost anything. To get specialist debt advice, ask if a trained debt adviser is available at the bureau. If not, there will be one at a nearby centre or at one of the money advice units run under the Citizens Advice banner. The adviser will help you write to creditors, construct a budget and prepare documents for court hearings if necessary.

Elaine Drummond, 24, was a lone parent living in South Wales with her three children when she visited a local debt advice charity. She was referred to the CAB for advice on multiple debts, one of which was a credit card issued by a high street bank. The credit card was offered to her when she called into the branch to pay some bills - it appears the bank was having a promotion on credit cards. There was no evidence that the bank had carried out a credit check or written agreement. Her only income was her weekly income support payments. She was sent a card in the post with a credit limit of £3,500. She used £2,500 credit on the card but had no prospect of repaying this sum. She lived in rented accommodation and was recommended to declare herself bankrupt.

NATIONAL DEBTLINE

Another organisation that has received a boost from the government in recent years, National Debtline is a specialist service that dispenses advice over the phone. A few facts about the charity:

- It dealt with more than 270,000 debt queries last year.
- It sends callers its self-help information pack 'Dealing with your debts'.
- It is funded by grants from the Department of Trade & Industry and the major banks.
- It refers clients that need a DMP to either the Consumer Credit Counselling Service or Payplan (see opposite).

National Debtline is a good source of information that is available immediately. Its focus on debt also means that all its staff understand exactly the issues that you are facing.

❝ National Debtline provides information packs and refers clients who need a DMP on to other agencies. ❞

To find your nearest CAB, go to www.adviceguide.co.uk. Visit the National Debtline website at www.nationaldebtline.co.uk or call 0808 808 4000.

CONSUMER CREDIT COUNSELLING SERVICE (CCCS)

The CCCS is well known for providing advice to hundreds of thousands of people each year who are struggling with debts. A few facts about the service:

- In 2006, the average debt of its clients was £31,370.
- It answered 293,000 calls on its freephone helpline (see box, below) – up 50 per cent on 2005.
- Of that number, 73,000 required an in-depth study of their finances.

If you have given up trying to persuade your creditors to accept a repayment plan, you can ask the CCCS to do it for you. Each year it devises thousands of debt management plans (see pages 136–8), which it administers for clients. It also administers individual voluntary arrangements (see pages 147–50), but says it does all it can to steer clients away from formal arrangements to the less formal debt management plan.

PAYPLAN

Payplan offers debt management plans free to the consumer because it is funded by the credit industry. A few facts about the trust:

- It started in 1999 on the basis that 'charging those with financial difficulties for a debt repayment service was fruitless, as it would take them even longer to become debt free and just compounded the problem'.
- It says that while it receives donations from the credit industry, it remains impartial and deals with all creditors – not just the ones that donate.
- It has a sister company, The Payplan Partnership, that handles individual voluntary arrangements.

The monthly payments that you make into your arrangement will cover the payments to your creditors as well as their fees for putting together and supervising the arrangement.

Payplan works closely with charities such as National Debtline.

MONEY ADVICE CENTRES

The recent explosion in the number of 'advice centres', both on the high street and online, must have led to confusion for many indebted people seeking help and support. While most advice centres

 Visit the CCCS website at www.cccs.co.uk or call Freephone 0800 138 111 or go to the Payplan website at www.payplan.com or call 0800 917 7823 (8am-9pm).

> **!** As with all advice, including the advice offered by the charities above, it is important to ask about fees and charges. If you find it confusing, call one of the helplines above. Don't assume that the friendly face on the other side of the counter is giving you independent advice.

will be run buy local charities, others use names that make them sound charitable, but are, in fact, profit-making businesses.

To find a local advice centre, contact CAB (see box at foot of page 140). You can also look in local telephone directories under 'Debt', but you will find it hard deciding which organisations are there to offer independent advice.

THE UK INSOLVENCY HELPLINE

A national group of insolvency lawyers and accountants set up this helpline (see box, below) in answer to what they called 'a huge influx of unregulated debt counsellors and debt management companies that had began trading in the last decade'.

The helpline has rapidly become the largest professional network of lawyers and accountants specialising in money advice in the UK. They are regulated by

their own professional bodies, unlike money advice staff working for private businesses, who are largely unregulated. It exists 'to promote the provision of independent money advice from the UK's regulated professional bodies'.

DEBT ADVICE COMPANIES

These are privately run firms that have damaged their reputations by imposing exorbitant fees and by making exaggerated claims that their powers of negotiation can reduce your debt by 80 or 90 per cent. Unfortunately, to the untrained eye, private debt advice firms look like charitable organisations. Most will claim the charities mentioned above are amateurish when it comes to negotiating with banks and that they can negotiate bigger cuts in your debts and minimise your repayments. In reality, there is little evidence to support this argument.

Some are reputable and offer independent advice. Others have made huge profits channelling their 'clients' (people in debt) to opt for one route only – the individual voluntary arrangement (IVA). This is discussed in depth in the following chapter. All we need to say here is that IVAs are expensive and make huge profits for those firms that recommend them.

 To find out more, go to the UK Insolvency Helpline website at www.insolvencyhelpline.co.uk or call 0800 074 6918.

Bankruptcy and insolvency

In this chapter we will examine what happens when you are insolvent and what choices are open to you. We will show that an individual voluntary arrangement (IVA) is a last resort, just like bankruptcy, and that it is not the easy option portrayed in television adverts by the IVA industry.

Dealing with insolvency

Nothing tells the story of Britain's new debt culture better than the rise in personal insolvencies. In 2006, there were 110,000 people who declared themselves financially bust. Around 45,000 of the 110,000 personal insolvencies opted for bankruptcy. The other 65,000 chose an individual voluntary arrangement (IVA).

This was a 39 per cent rise on the year before. It was an astonishing jump and when the figures were published, they sparked much hand wringing by politicians and social commentators. Why were so many people drowning in debt and what forces were dragging them under?

The rise of the IVA in recent years has proved particularly controversial. The Consumer Credit Counselling Service (CCCS) says it has seen a strong rise in the number of thirty- and forty-somethings choosing to solve their debt problems with an IVA. It says that many people opt for an IVA because they see it as a way to escape debts without repercussions. They believe it will let them keep their biggest assets – a home and car – and reduce their debts without any side effects. An IVA, they believe, also saves them from bankruptcy and the stigma that is still attached to it. Yet for many people, an IVA is probably the wrong choice (see pages 147–50).

A survey for the CCCS showed that more than half of its clients who were recommended bankruptcy rejected the

Jargon buster

Bankruptcy Dates back 300 years and has undergone several reforms, most recently in the 2002 Enterprise Act, which came into force in 2004. This brought in the one-year discharge from bankruptcy for individuals with credit debts, a cut from the previous two or three years. It also brought in an extended period of bankruptcy for people who were caught acting in bad faith or just plain crooks hell bent on defrauding their creditors

Insolvency This is the catchall phrase for someone who cannot pay their debts and cannot agree an informal repayment plan with their creditors. There are two main routes for the insolvent person to take – both are forms of bankruptcy and have been established by the government as legal contracts that the debtor and creditor must abide by

idea. The largest group cited stigma as the main reason.

WHO BECOMES INSOLVENT

Debt advisers say many people who become insolvent have suffered a financial shock. It might follow a serious illness, losing their job, separation or divorce. And when it happens, the financial consequences are dramatic, leading to a spiral of debt that can end in bankruptcy or the taking on of an IVA just at the point when their emotional problems are at their worst. They pay little attention to the legal process and the choices open to them and they accept what is recommended, failing to understand the consequences. It is usually a once-in-a-lifetime experience and that means they probably know very little about the choices open to them, or the rules and the jargon that surrounds the subject.

Before explaining how to handle your affairs when you go bust, it is worth saying that the best option is always to take on an informal arrangement with your creditors. It cannot be said enough times that formal arrangements, particularly an IVA, involve large fees and strict rules that can make matters worse (see the box, below).

When you consider insolvency as a solution to your debt problems, you need to ask yourself whether you have tried everything to cut your debt payments.

- **Are your loans, credit cards and mortgages** on the lowest possible interest rates?
- **Have your outgoings** been cut to the bone?
- **Have you claimed all the benefits** to which you are entitled?
- **Have you increased your income** as far as you are able?

The cost of an IVA versus bankruptcy

Fees to firms that recommend IVAs can be as much as £7,000. This can comprise an up-front fee of £1,500 and a retention fee of £1,000 a year for five years. The fees are paid for by creditors, who may have allowed bigger cuts in your payments if they weren't paying a fee.

Bankruptcy fees consist of a £150 court fee and a £335 deposit to help meet the official receiver's costs. If you are on means-tested benefits, you are exempt from the court costs, but will get no help with the deposit fee.

 The pros and cons of an IVA are covered on page 148 and the pros and cons of bankruptcy are covered on page 160. Read them to help you decide which is the best course of action for your circumstances.

If the answer to all these questions is yes (no matter how much you re-examine your finances) and there isn't enough money to pay bills and debts, then seek advice because insolvency might be the only next possible step.

If you can pay your mortgage or rent but have allowed personal loans, credit cards and other unsecured debts to get out of control, you need to negotiate or find someone who can negotiate on your behalf. Your creditors may understand that they need to negotiate to get any of their funds back when you have run out of money. You need to talk to them about your income and outgoings and make your creditors realise that there is only a small amount of cash available each month in order to pay debt bills. If, however, your creditors reject your attempts to negotiate, then pay what you can afford. If you simply don't have any money left, then bankruptcy is probably the only option.

❝ Talk with your creditors and see if you can negotiate paying what you owe in instalments. If they refuse, bankruptcy is the only solution. ❞

 See pages 136-8 for more details about negotiating an informal agreement, otherwise known as a debt management plan or DMP.

Applying for an IVA

Some debt advisers will judge cases on a sliding scale of debt and offer solutions, depending on how bad the situation has become: informal arrangements for smaller sums, all the way up to bankruptcy for the worst cases. But everybody's story is different. If you are struggling to cope, then seek independent free advice. Don't jump into the arms of an IVA company. IVAs are only for a minority.

An IVA is a legally binding agreement with unsecured creditors. It will allow you to pay as much as you can afford of your bank overdraft, credit card balances and outstanding personal loans. Payments to your unsecured creditors are made over five years (60 months).

IVAs have been around since 1986 and were designed to allow sole-trader businesses a way to avoid bankruptcy. They are essentially a way of making your 'best offer' to creditors. An IVA looks at your income compared with your necessary expenditure on housing, council tax, food, clothes, etc. Then a monthly payment proposal is made, and if 75 per cent of creditors vote to agree, it is legally binding on all of them.

Until 2004, around 5,000 people a year opted for an IVA. By 2006, they were all the rage and 65,000 people a year were choosing to repay debts using

one. How can this be, you might ask, when the CCCS recommends IVAs in only three per cent of cases and ten times that number are advised to take a debt management plan.

You can judge the benefits of an IVA by reading the pros and cons given on page 148.

> **❝** An IVA is a way of making your 'best offer' to creditors, proposing a monthly payment. If 75 per cent of them accept it, it becomes binding. **❞**

The differences between voluntary and involuntary bankruptcy are explained later in this chapter on pages 154-66.

The pros and cons of an IVA

Pros

- Agreement needed from only 75 per cent of creditors
- You make one payment per month
- You can negotiate to repay only a proportion of your debts
- You get to keep your home, but creditors can demand they keep any equity
- Because the agreement is legally binding, your creditors cannot ask for more money at a later stage
- From the date of approval, all interest and charges are frozen
- Unlike bankruptcy, your employer will not be made aware of the situation, but it does go on your credit file
- The IVA will overturn any county court judgements
- You can still re-mortgage your home when in an IVA, though creditors can still demand some or all of the money you have saved

Cons

- Claims by IVA firms that they can negotiate a cut in your debt of up to 80 per cent are misleading. The figure is more likely to be 30-40 per cent with 60 per cent at the most. The figure will depend on what you can afford according to the information you supply about your finances
- A rigid payment structure means that if you miss a payment by a few hours, your creditors can force you into bankruptcy
- The failure rate. So far, thousands of IVAs have collapsed because the agreed payments haven't been maintained, with the prospect that many more will fail following the boom in IVA sales in the last two years
- If your partner has some debts held jointly with you, they will probably be asked to join the IVA

! Your payment is worked out on your income minus everyday expenses. As with a DMP, the amount left over is supposed to be what you can afford to pay, not what creditors are asking for as a monthly payment (or what you think should be the payment). You can renegotiate an IVA should you start finding it difficult to pay the monthly bill, but it is not easy. You could then slide into bankruptcy. Before signing an IVA, use a cash diary (see page 180) for at least a few months to determine how much you spend. The diary should give you a settled idea of your outgoings for you to use in your calculations of a fair amount to pay each month.

GOING FURTHER

The first contact with an IVA company is usually by phone, when the adviser should discuss whether or not an IVA is appropriate.

- **The company sends you an information pack** requesting all the details of your debts, income and household expenditure.
- **On the basis of this information** it prepares a proposal to put to your creditors, suggesting exactly how much you can afford to pay. The IVA company usually takes about a month to negotiate with your creditors.
- **Once it has agreement from 75 per cent of the creditors by value (who vote),** you will have protection against your creditors charging further interest and taking court action. The creditors are not allowed to contact you after the agreement has been set up. The only person who can contact you is the insolvency practitioner. But if more than 25 per cent hold out against the deal, the IVA will fail without further effort by the insolvency practitioner in charge of your case.
- **Once you have signed the IVA,** as with a DMP, you make one payment per month under a private agreement. If your fear of bankruptcy is the public humiliation, an IVA is also a private agreement. As one debt management company says in its literature: 'Your name **does not** go in the local paper. You **do not** lose your home. You **do not** pay interest.' However, you may have to raise money against the equity.

- **Part of the agreement is regular monthly payments** at an appointed time. You must, however, make sure regular payments are made for 60 months. Minimum payments on an IVA tend to be £200–£300. Once an amount has been agreed, a standing order is set up with your bank.

CHOOSING AN IVA OVER A DMP

Most debt management companies say you should only apply for an IVA if you have debts of £15,000–£18,000 or more, otherwise consider a DMP as an alternative debt solution. One IVA provider says that its typical client is someone on £20,000 a year but with £46,000 in credit card and loan debt on top of their mortgage. 'They are not necessarily poor people but people who have just borrowed too much,' the company said.

But there are no rules as to the size of your debt when deciding on taking an IVA or a DMP. While they are probably correct to say that an IVA is not worth considering if your debts are less than £15,000, they are wrong to say that an informal arrangement should not be considered for sums over £15,000. All your unsecured debts, whether they amount to £5,000 or £50,000 can be sorted out informally with banks and credit companies.

Of course, with an informal agreement, there is the threat that it can be overturned at any time. Creditors can ask for more if they judge you are capable of paying more.

CHOOSING AN IVA OVER BANKRUPTCY

Those discharged bankrupts who have written about their experiences, and not many have, say the euphoria of escaping debts soon turns sour when they realise the restrictions on getting overdrafts, loans and mortgages prevent them establishing a normal life for several years.

Yet for many people who have a low income and large debts, an IVA can mean crippling levels of repayments for five years. Paying off your debts over this time, if it soaks up all your spare income, will be an even bigger barrier to getting new forms of credit.

The Bankruptcy Association, an independent debt advice group, says many people who have opted for IVAs should have opted for bankruptcy instead. It believes the growth of IVAs has failed to serve insolvent individuals who are often wrongly advised to opt for an IVA when they would be better off with a more informal arrangement or bankruptcy when their circumstances are more extreme.

WHEN DOES AN IVA OR DMP BECOME IMPOSSIBLE?

Using a DMP or IVA, you could cut into your debt mountain as follows, making it something you can afford:

- **If you have debts of £25,000,** you could reduce them to £16,500 and pay £275 per month.
- **If you have debts of £40,000,** you could reduce them to £19,500 and pay £320 per month.
- **If you have debts of £80,000,** you could reduce them to £32,400 and pay £540 per month.

But what if you don't have £275 spare at the end of each month, let alone £540? What if you have suffered such a financial shock, either from separation, divorce, a long illness or unemployment, that you have less than £100 a month to pay debt bills? At this point you need to consider bankruptcy and seek advice.

❝A DMP or IVA can land you with crippling levels of repayments for five years. ❞

To find out more about the Bankruptcy Association, which provides such things as telephone and letter advice, newsletters and contacts for specialist insolvency lawyers, go to www.theba.org.uk.

Using an IVA company

There are several consistent messages running through this book and one of them is to avoid doing business with IVA companies, most of which have sprung up in the last couple of years to advise the growing number of people with large debts.

The adverts are tempting because they promise to cut your debt dramatically – sometimes by 80 per cent or more. But IVA companies can be swayed in the advice they give by commercial considerations. For instance, it won't pay them to recommend an informal deal with creditors, which brings no fees and charges. They are not duty bound to give the best advice.

In response to the criticism, the industry has produced 'good practice' guidelines and many of the larger debt management companies have signed up to show that they are responsible at handling customer queries about bankruptcy and debt management.

A cynic might say that IVA companies, even the not-for-profit ones, will continue to steer you away from informal and largely unprofitable arrangements to more formal debt management plans. They will point out the main flaw of an informal plan, which is that lenders can return at a later stage and demand a higher payment rate. In reality, while lenders do pursue debtors for more money, you can keep them at bay with an informal plan. You are much more likely to inform them that you cannot keep up payments than the lenders are to say you are not paying back enough.

❝ The reality is that you can keep lenders who are pursuing you for more money at bay with an informal plan. ❞

WHO DO YOU TRUST?

The essential problem for anyone with serious debt problems is that the IVA companies and fee-paying debt management groups, whether they are not-for-profit organisations or a private company, earn commission and annual fees from managing IVAs and, to a lesser extent, DMPs. Informal arrangements don't generate any profits.

Some of these companies are highly profitable organisations listed on the stock market and have shareholders who want higher profits each year. The shareholders want to see the management maximising the return on their investment. In the debt management world, many suspect that this pressure results in them recommending the overly indebted buy an IVA when other options would be cheaper or more appropriate.

There are, however, also fee-charging, not-for-profit debt management companies. These firms say that because they don't have shareholders encouraging them to increase profits, they are under little pressure to sell IVAs to anyone who doesn't want one. But they are not charities. They must pay their staff and, in the case of the boss, that can be quite a large amount.

Some of the debt management firms have spent many thousands of pounds advertising how they play fair by customers and never recommend a solution for their own profit, but it is almost impossible to determine which company is an 'honest John' from the greedy ones preying on unsuspecting debtors. For instance, it took action by the Advertising Authority and Office of Fair Trading before eye-grabbing daytime TV adverts were banned from promising customers they will pay back as little as 10 per cent of their debts. The adverts can still be aired. It's just they can't make such exaggerated claims.

You may satisfy yourself that a company advertising in the Yellow Pages or a local newspaper is a reputable firm based on a recommendation from a friend or family member. It is more likely, though, that you will receive a more independent service from one of the larger debt charities. The Consumer Credit Counselling Service, one of the largest debt charities, will often recommend a DMP.

It isn't known if the huge growth in IVAs and to a lesser extent DMPs is due to the fees advisers can earn, but there are many in the debt industry who believe it is only human nature to recommend the most profitable course of action. Therefore, charities that are largely government funded, such as Citizens Advice Bureau and National Debtline along with other independent charities such as Payplan, should be the first port of call for anybody in financial trouble (see pages 139–42).

Up-front costs

A large part of the fee charged by IVA providers is taken at the beginning of the plan, so it is not uncommon for the first 12 months of repayments to be taken up solely by the company's fees. National Debtline says one case shows very clearly how people can be worse off. A woman living in a rented council house entered into an IVA after seeing an advert in her local phone book. Her debts were £21,000. Two years later she has paid £9,000 into her IVA, £7,000 of which has been taken in fees.

The firms claim the thousands of pounds they earn in arrangement and management fees are paid by the lenders and not by the customers. The firms pretend their fees are free money when it is either added to your debts or is money the bank may have agreed to waive from your debts under a different deal.

In many ways, fee-charging debt management firms and IVA companies are cousins of estate agents. They sell themselves as hard business organisations that will bargain on your behalf more than a charity employee might do. You might not like them very much, but you would rather have them on your side bashing the banks into shape than the banks attacking you to pay your debts. However, there is a flaw to this basic sales pitch: the lenders are harder than they used to be. Where once they would allow an IVA company to push down debts to 10p in the £1, now many of them refuse to go below 40p in the £1 if the negotiator is an IVA firm with a reputation for luring customers with exaggerated claims.

❝ Much of the fee charged by IVA providers is taken at the beginning of the plan, sometimes taking up the first year's payments. ❞

Case Study — Mr and Mrs Neald

Mr Neald left teaching to start a small business. But the business was never profitable and, indeed, his accountant established that his losses were in excess of £50,000 in the first few months of trading. Mr Neald responded to an advertisement in a local paper, placed by an IVA company. They requested a fee of £1,500, which he paid. The company then referred Mr Neald to one of the largest firms of insolvency practitioners in the country. As Mrs Neald had borrowed funds in her name to assist her husband's business, it was recommended by the insolvency practitioner that they put forward a joint IVA proposal. Monthly payments ranging from £750 in the first year to £1,250 in the fifth year were to be made. A bank overdraft of around £15,000 was excluded from the arrangement. The payments were unsustainable and the couple are now bankrupt.

The Bankruptcy Advisory Service, which was founded in 1997 by insolvency practitioner Gill Hankey to advise people 'struggling with severe financial problems', says it learnt that Mrs Neald had never met or discussed her situation with either the fee-charging debt management firm or the insolvency practitioner. She merely signed a document put in front of her by her husband.

 To find out more about the Bankruptcy Advisory Service, go to www.bankruptcyadvisoryservice.co.uk or telephone: 01482 633034/5.

Bankruptcy

You can either choose to become bankrupt and bring your own bankruptcy petition or a creditor (or group of creditors) can force you into bankruptcy if you can no longer pay your debts.

VOLUNTARY BANKRUPTCY

The advantage of bankruptcy (compared to an IVA or DMP) is that once you have been granted a bankruptcy order, you can start again clear of debts. If you have reached an insurmountable problem with your levels of debt and can't see any other way out of it, you might want to consider taking a voluntary bankruptcy by bringing your own **bankruptcy petition**. To do this you'll need to consider taking the following steps:

- **Find out which court to go to.** This will usually be the county court in the area where you have lived for the last six months (although it can sometimes be where you work). In London, it is the High Court in the Strand. Any local county court or the High Court will tell you which is the right court for you.
- **Make sure you have enough money** for the deposit (£335). You won't get this back. There may also be a fee of £150, although depending on your circumstances, the court may reduce this amount or say that you don't have to pay it at all. Ask the court for form EX160, which tells you more about finance, or download it from Her Majesty's Courts Service website (see box, below).
- **Get hold of a bankruptcy petition** (form 6.27) and **statement of affairs** (form 6.28). Copies are available from your local court or from the Insolvency Service website (see box, opposite bottom), where you can either download the forms or fill them in online.
- **Fill in the forms.** You must list all your creditors, even if the debt is disputed. You must also give details of all your bank account and building society accounts. You will be asked to list other assets and items with a re-sale value, for example, a car and antiques.
- **Take the forms with two copies,** the

 To download form EX160 from the internet, go to www.hmcourts-service.gov.uk/infoabout/fees/exemption/ex160.htm

fee and the deposit to court, and swear an **affidavit**. This means that you swear to the court you have told the truth in the forms.

- Once you have sworn your forms, the court may either fix a time for the hearing or hear your case straightaway. If your case is in the county court, you will have to attend the hearing.

> **❝** Once you have been granted a bankruptcy order, you can start again clear of debts. If you can no longer pay your debts, you can opt for this yourself. **❞**

Case Study | **Beryl and Stan Collinson**

Beryl and Stan Collinson lived in Leicestershire in a modest house with their two adult children. To maintain their lifestyle, they accumulated numerous debts. They owned their own home and had secured borrowing totalling £160,000, made up of a mortgage and three loans. The property was valued and they found they were in negative equity – their lender had lent them more than the property was worth. After receiving money advice from Citizens Advice, they decided to petition for bankruptcy.

To repay the debts on the £160,000 of borrowings would have taken the couple, in their late fifties, beyond their retirement age. Even a reduced sum would have taken years.

While Beryl and Stan didn't want to lose their home, their only chance of retaining some of their income (rather than spending it on debt repayments), was to go bankrupt and rent a home nearby.

 Copies of the bankruptcy petition and statement of affairs forms are available at your local court or from the Insolvency Service website: www.insolvency.gov.uk/forms /forms.htm. Or telephone their helpline: 0845 602 9848

Jargon buster

Affidavit A sworn witness statement

Bankruptcy petition An application to the county court for bankruptcy proceedings to start. Can be requested by either a debtor wishing to make themselves bankrupt or a creditor pursuing a debtor

Bankruptcy restriction order (or undertaking) Additional restrictions on bankrupts whose conduct is considered to have been dishonest or blameworthy

Income payments agreement The official receiver or trustee in bankruptcy can ask you to agree to make regular payments to your creditors for three years from your income. It can demand more than half your disposable income

Income payments order If you fail to agree an income payment after bankruptcy, the official receiver can order you to pay and tell your employer to deduct the money from your salary

Insolvency practitioner An authorised person who specialises in insolvency, usually an accountant or solicitor. They are authorised either by the Insolvency Service or by one of a number of recognised professional bodies

Insolvency Service Government agency that advises on insolvency, regulates the insolvency industry and oversees the official receiver

Official receiver An officer of the court and civil servant employed by the Insolvency Service, who deals with bankruptcies and compulsory company liquidations

Statement of affairs A form sent by the court asking you to give details about your financial situation and the reasons for the bankruptcy

Winding up order Order of a court, usually based on a creditor's petition, for the compulsory winding up or liquidation of a company or partnership

 If you make false statements or don't tell the official receiver about all your property, this is a criminal offence and you could be fined or sent to prison. It is also a criminal offence to conceal property or documentary evidence, or to get rid of property before you go bankrupt (see box, opposite).

Selling your assets in advance of bankruptcy

If you sell your assets and still file for bankruptcy you could be prosecuted for deceiving the court about your true financial position. There are examples of people who sold all their valuable possessions and hid the proceeds from their creditors. They then filed for bankruptcy, telling creditors they had nothing of value for them to reclaim. Selling your home and possessions is usually spotted and prosecuted.

But if you sell your assets to avoid bankruptcy altogether, then it is a perfectly legitimate part of your own debt management plan. And if you subsequently become bankrupt after settling debts with the proceeds of these sales, it can also be seen by the court as a valid attempt to pay back creditors.

INVOLUNTARY BANKRUPTCY

We have discussed how you can file for bankruptcy when you run out of money to pay debts, but there are also occasions when a creditor forces you into bankruptcy. This occurs when one of your creditors serves a statutory demand, asking for payment within three weeks. The amount of money in dispute must be more than £750, though creditors can combine their debts to get over the £750 threshold. If your debts are anything like this small, they will most likely negotiate a settlement, if only because they must pay a 'petition cost' of £400 and court fees of £190.

If, after three weeks, you haven't paid, the creditor then files a bankruptcy petition against you to the county court. If creditors have already succeeded in getting county court judgements against you and already sent bailiffs to seize goods – unsuccessfully – they can skip the three-week statutory demand period.

❝ Involuntary bankruptcy occurs when a creditor serves a statutory demand asking for payment within three weeks. ❞

The bankruptcy petition is served by a 'process server' and the petition will have the specific amount you owe on the form. You should also see a 'statement of truth' signed by the creditor verifying that you owe them money.

If there is still a chance that you can pay your debts, you can do so before the bankruptcy hearing, which usually happens a few weeks after the petition is agreed by the judge. Furthermore, a bankruptcy hearing can be delayed a few weeks if you can show there is a good chance of raising the money in that time.

A judge needs to agree that the demand in the petition is a legitimate course of action. It is a technical point, but it is the court that decides you are bankrupt and not your creditors. The judge can delay a ruling on your bankruptcy if someone disputes the debt. It is not normally necessary for you to attend the bankruptcy hearing.

Disputing a bankruptcy petition

You might, for example, believe you don't owe the debt that is outlined in a bankruptcy petition or you believe the debt is unfair. For example, debt advisers have accused lenders of inflating debts with excessive interest payments, penalties and surcharges.

There is no doubt that disputing a petition is a difficult process. Convincing a court that a reputable lender has misled the court about the amount you owe or that it has artificially inflated the amount you owe, is always going to be an uphill struggle. If you can't afford legal representation at the court hearing, which is quite likely, you must ask a friend to support your case or do it yourself.

❝ Technically, the court decides you are bankrupt, not your creditors. ❞

Case Study Patrick Cullinane

An illustration of how difficult it can be to dispute a bankruptcy order is the much-publicised case of Patrick Cullinane, a scene shifter at Pinewood Studios. He was accused by the Inland Revenue (now HMRC) of owing £67,000 in unpaid income tax, despite earning at most £18,000 a year.

Mr Cullinane disputed the claim and continues to fight against the 'injustice' of his bankruptcy to this day. He was accused of working without declaring income for tax and also renting out rooms in his house without declaring income for tax.

After a drawn-out fight to try to prove that the accusations were false, Mr Cullinane was made bankrupt in 2000. The official receiver passed the Mr Cullinane case to insolvency practitioners at KPMG, one of the largest and most expensive tax advisers in the country.

The Inland Revenue, without explanation, reduced its claim from £67,000 to £38,000 prior to the bankruptcy hearing. In the end it only managed to get £18,000 from the sale of Mr Cullinane's assets. The costs of the bankruptcy are set out below:

Official receiver's disbursements	£527.35
Mortgage redemption	£26,128.19
Cheque/payable order fees	£7.80
Secretary of State fees	£10,313.23
Petitioner's costs	£2,188.66
Trustee's fees	£32,306.65
Trustee's expenses	£2,800.21
Irrecoverable VAT	£10,229.66
Agents/valuers' fees	£8,886.22
Agents' fees	£1,765.17
Legal fees	£13,749.25
Other property expenses	£15.00
Insurance of assets	£54.43
Inland Revenue preferential claim	£393.87
Inland Revenue unsecured claim	£17,634.31
Total:	**£127,000.00**
Receipts from property:	**£127,000.00**
Balance:	**Nil**

Mr Cullinane's house was sold for £127,000, but the mortgage of just over £26,000 had to be deducted from its selling price. The Inland Revenue, the only creditor, took less than £18,000. The rest of the money was eaten up in fees. In fact, KPMG's bill was almost double the £34,000 it took from the bankruptcy, but it was forced to take a cut in order to pay the creditor and other fees.

Mr Cullinane was forced into bankruptcy because he disputed the claim, but if the Inland Revenue had told him it would settle for less than £18,000, he might have been able to raise it one way or another.

The pros and cons of bankruptcy

Pros

- Pressure is taken off you because you don't have to deal with your creditors
- You are allowed to keep certain things, like household goods and a reasonable amount to live on
- When the bankruptcy order is over, usually after a year, you can make a fresh start. In some cases, this can be after only a few months
- Creditors must stop most types of court action to get their money back following a bankruptcy order (though there are still some cases when bailiffs may still be able to take your belongings away)
- If your house has been sold to pay debts, you may be able to apply to your local authority for re-housing
- The money you owe can usually be written off
- After discharge from bankruptcy you will be able to run your own business and act as a director of a company
- You can take out loans and mortgages, albeit at much higher than normal interest rates after being discharged

Cons

- Your own home will most likely be sold
- Until you are discharged from bankruptcy (usually within the first year), you will be obliged to declare you are an undischarged bankrupt when applying for credit in excess of £500
- Some of your possessions might have to be sold, for example, you will usually lose your car and any luxury items you own
- Some professions, such as accountants and lawyers, don't let people who have been made bankrupt carry on working
- If you own a business, it is more than likely that the official receiver will close down your business, dismiss your employees and sell off the assets
- It will cost you money (up to £485) to go bankrupt
- Going bankrupt can affect your immigration status
- You cannot keep your bankruptcy private. A list of bankrupt people is published on the internet and your case could also be published in your local newspaper
- If you failed to co-operate with the court or official receiver, you could have another order, called a bankruptcy restriction order made against you (see box, page 163)
- You may be subject to an income payment agreement (see below)
- Any member of your family or even your employer, could be publicly examined in court if the official receiver believes this will aid the investigation
- Even when you are no longer bankrupt, there are some debts, such as court fines and student loans, that will never be written off. In the case of student debt, repayments will be deducted whenever you earn above £15,000 (see page 79). Unpaid court fines will appear on your credit file, harming your ability to apply for credit

WHAT HAPPENS WHEN YOU BECOME BANKRUPT?

At the bankruptcy hearing, the court will decide either to reject your (or your creditor's) application, or to make a bankruptcy order. The court will reject the application if, for example, they think there is a better solution to your debt problem. Once the bankruptcy order is made, all your bank and building society accounts will usually be frozen immediately and you will lose control of your other main assets. Your money will come under the control of the **official receiver**, who is an employee of the government-run **Insolvency Service** and works from one of around 40 offices across Britain. You should try to make sure you have enough cash for day-to-day expenses before your accounts are frozen (see 'Your bank account' box on page 169).

If there are few assets, the receiver may handle the case itself. It will most likely pass it on to a third party if there is a property or other large asset to sell. The third party will usually be an insolvency practitioner working for a firm of accountants or a specialist insolvency practice.

The official receiver or insolvency practitioner will arrange an interview with you. After your interview, the official receiver will tell your creditors about the bankruptcy, and send them a report with a summary of your financial situation. Your assets will be sold to pay the insolvency practitioner's bills for handling the case. The remainder will be sent to your creditors. Sometimes creditors receive very little of their money from a bankruptcy.

Your spouse's assets

If you have a joint bank account with your spouse, then that will be frozen along with your own personal bank and building society accounts. Your spouse needs to open a separate account before you are made bankrupt and should take legal advice on keeping as many assets in his or her hands as possible.

Ask the expert

How does the insolvency practitioner know what assets exist?

After the bankruptcy order has gone through, the official receiver will ask for an interview. He or she will ask for details of your bank accounts and other information. An agent will most likely be sent to your home, or business address if you are self-employed, to seize assets. Seizure of assets and bank accounts, any investments and other assets can be very rapid in the aftermath of bankruptcy.

If you own a home or have a mortgage on a home, the property will be taken by the creditors; you can't sell the house yourself once you are declared bankrupt and use the money to buy a smaller home. The sale could happen up to three years after the date of your bankruptcy. You and your family will be allowed to live there for at least a year, but during that time you are expected to make other arrangements to move your family to rented accommodation. After one year, there is no protection against the home being sold.

Don't think you will get change out of the insolvency practitioners who handle the sale. Even if the equity in the home is worth much more than you owe, you will almost certainly lose the lot (see the Mr Cullinane case study on page 159).

You will also be forced to give up your car, unless it is worth less than £2,500. If you have a valuable antiques collection, collection of pedigree dogs or valuable collection of tools (see small business debts, pages 164–5), these could also be sold by the administrator of your bankruptcy.

It is also only in exceptional circumstances that your household items are going to attract any attention unless they are of such a value that the sale of the item would raise a significant amount of money to pay to your creditors. For example, if you have recently purchased a large LCD flat screen television, then that could be seized, while an old cathode ray tube television will be virtually worthless. The same principle works for PCs. Costume jewellery is not of much value either, but if you possess valuable jewellery, it might be of interest to the official receiver.

Your pension fund falls outside the bankruptcy but your pension income could be claimed by the official receiver.

A bankruptcy order normally lasts one year, though it can be less if you have co-operated fully with the official receiver. The official receiver tells you when the bankruptcy order is completed.

If you rent your home

If you rent and have serious debts, then bankruptcy becomes a more obvious option. It will come as little surprise that most people who file for bankruptcy rent their accommodation. They will lose little from the bankruptcy except the restriction for a few years on getting out a new mortgage and other credit.

 For more information, contact the Insolvency Service, either through their website – www.insolvency.gov.uk – or call their insolvency helplne on 0845 602 9848.

LIFE AFTER BANKRUPTCY

The official receiver will tell you when the bankruptcy is over. Most debts that haven't been paid will then be written off.

One of the main issues confronted by bankrupts is the problems they have getting a bank account and credit after they have been discharged. Banks are less likely to forgive than the government and make life difficult for anyone who has defaulted on credit payments.

Most people who have a regular income will also be required to make monthly payments for three years towards their debts based on what the official receiver thinks they can afford. This is called an **income payment agreement** and is used to make you pay off more of your debts from spare income. If you don't have any spare income once your debts have been written off, then the receiver will leave you alone.

❝One of the main issues facing bankrupted people is the problems they have in getting a bank account and credit after they have been discharged.❞

A bankruptcy restriction order

If the official receiver or insolvency practitioner handling your bankruptcy believes you are to blame in some way for becoming insolvent or took on debts knowing that you had no hope of paying them back, he or she can issue a bankruptcy restriction order. It is a draconian rule that means you will have to ask the receiver before you don almost anything financial or in business life.

They can last for 15 years, and will make your financial affairs very restricted. If a bankruptcy restriction order is granted, you cannot become a Member of Parliament, act as a Justice of the Peace, be a governor of a school or become a member of the local authority. The bankruptcy order remains on your credit reference file for six years, restricting your access to credit for that period.

SMALL BUSINESSES AND INSOLVENCY

Businesses usually hit the rocks when their cash flow runs dry. You might have borrowed money to invest in the business and underestimated the impact of interest payments. Your customers might prove unable or unwilling to pay for goods already delivered. You might run a shop that faces a hike in rent or whopping tax bill. In each case, your business could run out of cash, leaving you unable to pay essential bills.

If your business is a limited company of which you are a director, creditors will be unable to pursue you for your property or personal belongings to get their money back. They must therefore look to the business and its assets. Even so, if you are a small business facing spiralling debts, you need to address the problem carefully because under UK law, the directors may be liable for wrongful trading if their company trades while insolvent. Directors can avoid liability for wrongful trading if they are able to prove that they took sufficient steps to minimise the loss to the creditors after realising that the company was insolvent.

Furthermore, a business large enough to have employees, plant and machinery or other assets needs to take expert advice to avoid losing everything in a bankruptcy. Also, staff will become creditors when their employer becomes insolvent and so they can pursue redundancy payments from the Redundancy Payments Office at the Insolvency Service.

Sole traders

A sole trader is not in the same position as the director of a limited company, but they are governed by the same rules.

❝ In a small business facing spiralling debts, the directors may be held liable for wrongful trading if the company trades while insolvent. ❞

 For more information on small-businesses see the *Which? Essential Guide Working for Yourself.*

Start by trying to negotiate

This is not a head in the sand moment ... you need to act swiftly. As discussed earlier, the best way to handle the situation is to approach your creditors and explain that you cannot afford to pay debts and interest payments and need to negotiate a solution (see pages 132–5). An IVA or DMP is the next best thing – see pages 147–50 and 136–8. As alternatives to bankruptcy, all three options have fewer consequences and may be more suitable for someone wishing to remain in business.

Is the only solution bankruptcy?

The Enterprise Act 2002 frees an indebted individual from their debts within 12 months of the bankruptcy order being made. During that period the bankruptcy is investigated, bankruptcy restrictions apply and assets are dealt with. Insolvency rules say you can keep basic items you need for your trade and home life. These include:

- Tools, books, vehicles and other items of equipment that you need to use personally in your employment, business or vocation.
- Clothing, bedding, furniture, household equipment and other basic items you and your family need in the home.

All these items must be disclosed to the official receiver who will then decide whether you can keep them.

Sole traders in the building and construction industry, one of the worst affected by insolvencies, report that the official receiver is sometimes quite harsh in its interpretation of the rules and leaves them without essential tools to carry on their trade. Probably for this reason alone DMPs and IVAs have become popular among sole traders and small businesses. A DMP/IVA is particularly appropriate for businesses that could return to profitability once their debt issues have been resolved. For instance if:

- The business is suffering from commercial debt.
- The company's losses are thought to be temporary.
- There has been an unexpected large expenditure.
- The company's financing facilities have been withdrawn.

If you are a sole trader, bankruptcy will result in the closure of your business. But it allows you to escape debts and be up and running again within a few months. Using an informal arrangement, DMP or IVA, you could be forced to continue paying large debts while running your business.

❝ Some sole traders in building and construction feel the official receiver can be harsh, leaving them without essential tools. ❞

Some other points that affect small businesses

- **A bankrupt cannot be a director** of a limited company until they are discharged. By contrast, an IVA/DMP does not prohibit an individual from continuing as a director.
- **A bankrupt cannot trade** under a different name in business without informing those with whom business is conducted of the trading name used when the bankruptcy order was made. A DMP or IVA will allow you to carry on in business using any trading name.
- **Bankruptcy may involve the loss of your house** and assets of significant value if you are a sole trader or in a partnership. Under an informal arrangement or IVA, you may be expected to release equity from your home if you have a mortgage, but the house will remain with the owner.

"A bankrupt cannot be a director of a limited company, and might lose their house and other assets if they are a sole trader or in a partership."

Courts and bailiffs

People who ignore demands from their creditors are heading for trouble. A county court judgement for non-payment of a debt can seriously damage your credit rating. It can also be a strong signal that you are not tackling your debts. In this chapter we look at what happens when your creditors make a claim, the arrival of bailiffs at your door and moves by lenders to file repossession orders.

Creditors and the courts

The first thing to say about any threat of court action is that you should seek advice. Even though most people chased by creditors to repay debts never see the inside of a court, there are forms to fill in and difficult concepts to grasp. The rules are complex and legal jargon is everywhere. It is much better to have the help of an adviser from one of the non-charging debt charities on your side.

Figures for the first three months of 2007 showed the number of creditors resorting to court action rather than negotiation to settle outstanding debt had reached a ten-year high. A total of 247,187 consumer debt-related county court judgements for non-payment cases were issued in the first three months of the year – the highest quarterly total since the summer of 1997.

Debt advisers blame the rise partly on the greater financial pressures on householders following a succession of interest rate rises. They also see it occurring partly due to a willingness by creditors to use the courts to reclaim money owed to them. Citizens Advice says it is concerned that creditors are using court action rather than trying to negotiate with debtors. 'Proposals to make charging orders easier to obtain may encourage them to do this even more in future,' it says.

> **❝ Some 70 per cent of county court judgements are issued in cases of failure to repay debts. ❞**

WHO IS PURSUED THROUGH THE COURTS?

County court judgements (also known as CCJs) are issued in cases of failure to repay debts to either an individual or a company. It is estimated that 70 per cent of judgements are credit related, with the rest issued by the Driver and Vehicle Licensing Agency, water companies and HM Revenue & Customs.

Despite the sharp rise, some debt advisers say they detect a sea change in attitude among some of the larger lenders, which can see that simply issuing more and more CCJs isn't going to get customers to repay loans when they simply haven't got any money. The courts also have a growing reputation for not only being costly (for both parties) but also ineffectual, especially when the outstanding debt is large.

These lenders are referring customers to debt advice charities to help them start the process of addressing debt problems. That leaves catalogue companies, store card operators and other lenders to make up a good slice

Jargon buster

Charging order This is a legal device giving an unsecured creditor a charge on your home. The creditor, such as a personal loan provider, effectively gives itself some security because you must then repay the loan from the proceeds if your home is sold

take the view that further down the line, if you refuse to pay, it can place a 'charging order' on your house. Placing a charge on your house effectively gives the creditor a slice of the equity in the house should it be sold. It knows that if the worst happens and you go bankrupt, it will have a good chance of getting its money back.

GET ADVICE

If you find yourself heading for court, you need to seek a free debt advice charity as the legal world can be a confusing place for the layman. At the time of writing, the government is seeking to make the process of the civil courts more easily understood by the public and the system more efficient at dealing with cases. In some instances, the new rules will make it easier for individuals to defend claims by creditors. Other rules in

of the rise in CCJ claims. They are often pursuing small debts, maybe £200–£300, which the lender believes can be recovered by the court, either by levying a fine or sending round bailiffs.

Lenders will almost certainly pursue you if you own a house. Even if you owe a relatively small amount, the lender will

Your bank account

One important detail before you start on the rocky road to court is your bank account. Whether your debt is with a credit card company, your bank or many creditors, it is best to pay whatever income you have into a separate account. Banks are liable to freeze accounts that you cannot maintain, and if you are unable to pay credit cards and mortgages, you are more than likely to have used up your overdraft facility.

Many debt advisers recommend using an internet current account so you can monitor your income and outgoings. Then

you can leave behind your overdraft and continue to pay debts.

If you use your existing bank account, you will put yourself at the mercy of your current bank who will insist you pay your overdraft first. Your bank needs to stand in line with all your other creditors. The earlier you do this, the better chance you have of then securing a mainstream account. If you leave it too late, you may be forced to accept a basic bank account, which lacks many of the facilities you will need to conduct your affairs easily (see pages 187–90).

the Tribunals, Courts and Enforcement Bill will make it easier for creditors to get their money back. The new rules are yet to gain Royal Assent and are still subject to many amendments.

How the court process affects you can depend on how your lender pursues the case. There are many tales of families arranging to appear in court to dispute a repossession order, for instance, only to find that the lender has asked for a delay, the court has failed to inform the family and the case is adjourned. The next hearing is arranged at another court many miles from the family home and at a difficult time for the family to attend. These tales show how you need to keep your wits about you – something that must seem almost impossible when court action over debts is threatened.

COURT PROCEEDINGS

It won't come as a surprise to most people that the legal system is complicated and potentially hazardous. The rules are so complicated that it is only possible in this chapter to give an outline of what can happen. For a comprehensive view, you should read *The Debt Advice Handbook*, published by Child Poverty Action Group (CPAG, 2006), which sets out the rules in much greater detail and can be found at most large libraries or good bookshops.

The basics

All claims arising from regulated credit agreements must be started in the county court, whatever their value.

Some time ago, the government made the system more efficient (especially for lenders with lots of defaulting customers), by establishing the Claim Production Centre (CPC) and the County Court Bulk Centre in Northampton. These centres deal with straightforward debt collection work, which is, in the main, undefended. The centres work in partnership with local courts and are intended to provide users with a faster service for a reduced court fee.

If you have defaulted on a credit agreement, the claim against you will almost certainly be processed and judged at Northampton.

The process

If we look at what happens in a standard case, you will get a sense of the process.

The normal method of taking someone to court is for the claimant to complete a form (not surprisingly called a claim form) and issue it at a county court. The claim can be issued in any county court (hence the growing dominance of Northampton). On receipt of the claim form, the court allocates a claim number and enters the details into

To read more about the OFT's guidance procedures, go to www.oft.gov.uk. Click on the 'Advice and resources' tab at the top of the home page and then follow 'Resource base' to 'Legal powers' to 'Consumer Credit Act' to 'Credit agreements' to 'Debt collection'.

the court's records. A response pack is attached to the claim form, which is then sent to the person being sued (in legal parlance, the claim is served on the defendant).

The defendant has a specific time in which to reply to the claim. During that time, a defendant can either pay the claim, dispute it (defend it), admit the claim and ask for more time to pay it or ignore it. If the claim is defended, a judge can treat it in several ways. The most informal is in the small claims section (below £5,000). Anything larger gets more attention from the judge.

If a defendant does not reply to the claim, the claimant can ask the court to enter judgement; that is, to make an order that the defendant pay the claim (judges in Northampton will make an order on hundreds of claims a day). If the defendant has admitted the claim and asks for more time to pay and the claimant accepts the offer, a request for judgement can also be made. If the judgement is ignored, it is open to the claimant to issue enforcement proceedings to obtain payment. Judgements and enforcement (bailiffs) are explained later in this chapter.

The defence offered by most defendants in court is usually to dispute the debt or to say the lender has acted unreasonably when it refused a payment plan. To put together a defence you will need advice from a free debt advice charity (see pages 139–42). Prior to the case, or during it, you can still offer to pay off the debt – in instalments you can afford – by filling in the forms the

court will send you. The court can also impose on the creditor your proposals for repayment.

All creditors and debt collection agencies have to follow the debt collection guidance laid down by the Office of Fair Trading (OFT) (see box, opposite). If they have failed to follow the guidance procedures, the court can find in your favour. This includes 'putting pressure on debtors or third parties which is considered to be oppressive'. If they fail to follow the rules, you can also complain to the debt collection agency, your local trading standards department and to the OFT.

Bankruptcy court proceedings

If the purpose of the court action is to go bankrupt, there is a different procedure you must follow, which is described on pages 154–63.

 Failure to comply with the repayment terms of a judgement will result in you being placed on the county court judgement register for six years, making it harder for you to take out a loan or mortgage.

Bailiffs and repossession

Some lenders are quick to escalate a debt problem and put it in the hands of a debt collection agency. These agencies are often prepared to accept a lower payment than the lender was asking you to find, but if the demand for repayment is still more than you can afford, you could find yourself opening your front door to bailiffs.

Regulations covering bailiffs, otherwise known as **enforcement agents**, are currently especially fragmented, says the government.

BAILIFFS

The role of the bailiff is to take your goods away and sell them to raise money to pay your creditors. Debt advisers recommend seeking their advice when bailiffs come knocking because the rules governing their behaviour are complicated. For instance, what bailiffs can take and how they can take it without breaking the law depends on what your debt is for. Bailiffs are commonly used when:

- You have council tax arrears.
- There is a county court judgement against you.
- There are unpaid fines.
- Child support payments are in arrears.
- Rent payments are in arrears.
- Income tax payments are in arrears.
- Parking penalties (fines) are overdue.

Bailiffs have a terrible reputation, which debt advice groups say is much deserved. Too often they exploit people's ignorance of the rules and use bullying tactics to get what they want. One study funded by Citizens Advice shows that 64 per cent of bailiffs are guilty of harassing and intimidating people, 40 per cent distort their powers of entry, 25 per cent threaten people with jail and 42 per cent charge excessive fees.

A government report says: 'While there are some elements within the industry that are quite strictly regulated, there are others that are only subject to informal regulation through trade associations, and others that appear to be subject to no regulation at all.' The report, which was written by civil servants, said there was a need 'for a more formalised structure to regulate the industry, which would raise standards of professionalism within the industry, and give the public greater confidence in it'.

This recognition from people close to the industry shows what individuals who have no money must deal with when they come up against bailiffs.

The government estimates there are 5,200 enforcement agents operating within England and Wales working for around 150 firms. There are:

- 600 county court bailiffs
- 1,600 other state-employed enforcement agents (such as tax collectors and customs officers)
- 200 local authority-employed enforcement agents
- 1,600 certificated private bailiffs
- 1,200 non-certificated private bailiffs.

Disturbingly, the government report says: 'In general terms, there is currently no formal complaints process for private enforcement agents.' Some firms belong to professional associations, which are independent from the government and have their own internal complaints and disciplinary procedures, so you must rely on their goodwill when you complain. The bailiffs charge fees according to a loose set of guidelines that individuals must challenge if they believe them to be excessive – seek advice to find out what is excessive. The fees can make up a huge part of any bill when they come to seize goods. Bailiffs can legally:

- Take your goods away only when they have a court order to do so.

Bailiffs can't legally:

- Break into your home. They can only gain entry if you invite them in or if they find an open window or open door when you are out.

They also work on the assumption that you will want to resolve the situation because bailiffs charge a fee for every visit they make to your home. The fees are set by the government, but it is widely recognised that bailiffs sometimes ignore these tariffs and set their own fees. So every time you turn them away, the debt gets bigger and the situation remains unresolved.

If they gain entry (legally), they will ask you to tell them how much of the contents is yours and what belongs to other people. If you do not respond, they can treat all the goods as yours. Remember, this is an 'act first, ask questions later' industry and if they do things you think are unreasonable or illegal, you will find yourself fighting after your belongings have long gone.

They should steer clear of bedding and basic clothing, furniture and household goods. Everything else can be taken for sale at auction, though the circumstances of your situation are crucial and there can be many exceptions. For example, if there are

Bailiffs' fees

Bailiffs instructed by county courts must levy fees according to a tariff structure. This should give debtors some comfort that their fees are fair, but they give a good deal of leeway for bailiffs to impose what many debtors believe are excessively high costs. Your debt adviser should scrutinise the fees to check if they are fair.

things belonging to someone else, then they must leave them alone, but if something is shared with your partner, they can take it. To recover rent arrears, they can take everything from a rented apartment.

If they agree to give you a few days to raise money and pay the debt, they will probably ask you to sign a 'walking possession agreement'. For a fee they will go away, but not until they have made a list of everything they want to take should you fail to pay the debt by a specified date.

Reporting harassment

What happens when you are one of the 60 per cent who suffer harassment and bullying at the hands of a bailiff? You can complain, though there are no statistics to show how successful complaining has been over the years. A bailiff should belong to a professional body, such as the Certificated Bailiffs Association, the Association of Civil Enforcement Agencies, the National Association of Investigators and Process Servers or the Enforcement Services Association see box opposite). When they call, you can ask which one they belong to. You can also complain to your creditors, to the court and to the police if they are threatening violence. If in doubt, seek expert help from a free debt advice service.

Complaining about fees charged by certificated or private bailiffs

If you think that the fees charged by them are too high, you can apply to the court for the fees to be taxed. This means that a district judge will decide if the fees you have been charged are reasonable or not. You should seek legal advice from a Citizens Advice Bureau,

 Enforcement agents are expected to comply with the guidelines laid down in the National Standards for Enforcement Agents, which you can find at the Department for Constitutional Affairs at www.dca.gov.uk/enforcement/agents02.htm.

solicitor or law centre before going to court – if you lose, you may then end up paying even more than your original debt.

Complaining about county court bailiffs

If you have a complaint against a county court bailiff, you should write to the court manager of the county court concerned. State your name, address, the case number, the warrant number and the facts about your complaint. The court manager will then investigate your complaint and write to you to inform you about what action will be taken.

Complaining about private bailiffs

You can complain about a private bailiff by telephoning or writing to the firm that the bailiff works for or the organisation who employed the bailiff to act on their behalf. Some of these organisations, such as HMRC, Customs and Excise and local authorities, have their own complaints procedures in place and information on how to complain can be obtained from their local offices.

The bailiff trade associations are responsible for promoting higher standards in the bailiff industry and will investigate your complaint.

HOME REPOSSESSION

Losing your home is a financial disaster. Even if you have only recently bought the property and have little equity to lose, the cost of buying a home is going up all the time and getting back on the property ladder becomes increasingly expensive.

If you have fallen behind with your monthly mortgage payments, you must contact your lender. As with all other debts, a head-in-the-sand attitude will only make things worse. Lenders have different policies towards their customers who fall into arrears. Some play strictly by the letter of the mortgage contract, others are more understanding.

Debt advisers report that lenders are increasingly reluctant to push for a repossession order because the courts don't like throwing people out of their homes, especially if there are other family members to consider. However, don't be complacent. In a rising property market, lenders can easily get their money back from selling your home and so will want to press for repossession if you appear reluctant to work through the problem with them. Even if you live away from the country's property hotspots, the lender could decide that getting back some of its money immediately is better than waiting. So you must act quickly. Consider the

 Website addresses for the bailiff professional bodies listed here are: www.naips.co.uk (National Association of Investigators and Process Servers), www.ensas.org.uk (Enforcement Services Association) and www.acea.org.uk (Association of Civil Enforcement Agencies).

following in an attempt to keep hold of your property:

- **Increase your income** from letting out a room and claiming on a mortgage payment protection insurance policy (see pages 119 and 95).
- **Reduce mortgage payments** for a fixed period by extending the time over which the mortgage is paid (see page 102).
- **Re-mortgage** to a cheaper deal (see pages 93–100).
- **Suspend an endowment** used to pay for some or all of the property (take advice from a financial adviser before making changes to an endowment policy) (see page 108).

Then there is the option of selling the property if you believe your financial problems will continue for the longer term.

❝ The way you deal with your mortgage lender will influence the judge should you come to court to fight a repossession of your home. ❞

Dealing with your mortgage lender

Keep in the back of your mind that the way you deal with your mortgage lender will influence a judge should the worst come to pass and you find yourself in court trying to prevent the repossession of your home.

Take the same approach to a mortgage lender as you would to any other lender:

- **Write a letter** to your mortgage lender and include a copy of your financial statement. Clearly set out your offer, which should comprise making regular payments, however small they may be. Even if your lender has yet to accept the offer, or indeed has refused it, it is another signal that you want to be helpful and will help your case should it come to court.
- **Show them a budget schedule** outlining your income and outgoings and where mortgage payments fit in (see pages 20–5).

If, after this approach, the lender is reluctant to support you, you should seek advice. You can threaten to take a complaint to the financial ombudsman (see box, page 196) saying that your complaint would focus on the poor response of the lender to offers from you to repay the loan.

 The Financial Services Authority (FSA) website has information about switching your mortgage at www.moneymadeclear.fsa.gov.uk.

If all else fails

If your finances have collapsed to the extent that you cannot put together a reasonable repayment plan, the court will then allow the lender to press ahead with a repossession order. The number of repossession applications have been steadily creeping up in recent years. Figures from the Department for Constitutional Affairs show that just under 30,000 repossession applications were made in the courts by lenders in the three months to the end of September 2006. This was a 55 per cent increase on the same period in 2004. On the plus side, only a fraction of borrowers ultimately had their homes repossessed. The department said out of 32,366 orders made in the first half of 2006, only 4,640 homes were actually repossessed.

When your lender sells the property, it will most likely be at auction. If the sale price fails to cover the mortgage, you will still be liable for the remainder. So the message that comes across loud and clear is that if you can see the situation arising where you can no longer furnish your mortgage, then it is always better to sell the property yourself and not allow the lender to sell in haste. You will get a better price and at least walk away with something. If there is equity in the property, you can keep it and if there isn't much equity, you are more likely to find a sale by the lender leaves you with a shortfall to make up.

Dealing with a second mortgage lender

If you have a secured loan on the property as well, the situation becomes even more complicated. A secured loan is called a second mortgage not only because you most likely took out the loan after the main mortgage, but also because the secured loan company stands in second place, behind the main mortgage lender, in the grab for your property assets.

The secured loan lender can push for the sale of your home if you fail to keep up payments on the loan, but will only get its money back after the main mortgage lender is satisfied.

> **!** Never hand back the keys to the mortgage lender – the mortgage and buildings insurance will remain in place and you will be liable to pay both until a sale is organised. As above, a sale by the lender is the worst possible scenario. A lender needs a court order before they can demand the keys.

❝ The number of repossession orders has been rising, but only a fraction of borrowers actually had their homes repossessed. ❞

CAR REPOSSESSION

If the car sitting outside your house was bought with a hire purchase (HP) contract and not a personal loan, the situation is delicate. An HP agreement is not a priority loan because the lender cannot pursue you to jail, but it will seem like a priority loan when the lender can take back your car.

Few people are happy to be without their car and many need it for work. So if you feel you are struggling with your car repayments, nip it in the bud and let the finance company know as soon as possible. The company will sometimes be able to help.

Your lender has the right to take back the goods without going to court if:

- You don't keep up your repayments.
- You have paid less than a third of the total cost of the HP agreement.
- Your car is parked in the road.

It depends on the type of lender you are dealing with as to whether they trigger repossession quickly or give you some time to kick-start repayments again. You will be sent a notice first, giving you the chance to put things right, but you will need to act quickly – within seven days.

If you haven't got the money to put things right and the lender won't agree to less than full payment, you could be heading for court. To repossess the car, the lender will have to go to court if:

- You have paid more than a third of the total cost of the HP agreement (not including any insurance).
- Your car is parked in your drive or at the home of a third party. Parking around the corner rarely works, according to debt advisers, because bailiffs always check the surrounding roads and side streets for the vehicle.

Courts cost money, so if you are having problems keeping up with repayments, it may be cheaper in the long run to hand the goods back. You can terminate an HP agreement and return the goods when you have paid up to half the original price (the exact amount will be stated in a box on the front of your contract).

❝ You can terminate an HP agreement and return the goods when you have paid up to half the original price, depending on the contract. ❞

Staying out of debt

Once you have agreed to pay back some or all of your debts, you need to organise your finances to make this as simple as possible. The worst possible result after months of negotiations and heartache would be for your agreement to fail after only a few months or even years. You want it to run the full course and to get rid of the problem.

Sticking to the plan

What sort of arrangement you have in place, determines the course of action that you will follow to maintain payments, but first it is good to have an understanding as to how you can keep to a budget.

KEEPING TO A BUDGET

There are hundreds of manuals and self-help books that provide techniques and advice about how to stick to a budget. It takes a little bit of grit and determination not to be blown off course by the desire to buy something or splash out on an unforeseen event. While most of them wrap up common sense in an expensive cover, their messages are usually simple and effective.

- **Keep a cash diary.** This is an extension of the budget you put together when you found yourself in financial trouble (see pages 20–5). Write down all your daily expenditure and keep it going for as long as possible – maybe for a few months. This will help keep your spending in check and help you see when your spending is more than your income can cope with.

- Alternatively, plan in a few treats. Keeping a close eye on your spending can become too miserable, so look out for free or low cost treats to make you feel alive while your debts are kept under control. Apply for free tickets to be in the audience for television and radio shows (see box, below). There are the free museums and art galleries to visit. Also visit your library to find out about free events in your area.

❝ A cash diary will itemise your daily expenditure and help you see when your spending is too high, keeping outgoings in check. ❞

To apply for tickets for television and radio shows, go to www.bbc.co.uk, www.itv.com or www.channel4.com and search for 'tickets'. There is a wide choice of programmes made across the country, so you don't only have to be London based to enjoy seeing some of your favourite shows being made.

INFORMAL REPAYMENTS

If you have an informal repayment arrangement, you will have letters from your creditors telling you what they expect you to pay each month. They might have insisted on repayment of the debt in full or a reduced amount, depending on your circumstances.

The payments could be spread over five years in monthly installments, like more formal arrangements such as an IVA, or a longer period because the debt was large or because you have requested a longer payment period to keep monthly bills low. To make the plan work:

- **Treat the arrangement** as a binding agreement.
- **Set up direct debits** or standing orders from a separate bank account to pay creditors (see basic bank accounts on pages 187–90).
- **Write down all your expenditure** and income for as long as possible. Keeping a household budget will allow you to see how much spare cash you have at the end of each month.
- **When creditors review the payments,** tell them to stick with the agreed arrangement.
- **If your income drops,** tell your creditors payments need to be cut too. Supply a new financial statement of income and outgoings.

Banks will usually want to review your repayments every six months. The level of curiosity about your financial situation varies from lender to lender. If they insist on recovering more of the debt through higher monthly payments, despite your protests, seek help from a debt adviser (see pages 139–42).

At some stage, you might want to pay more, but never rush to increase payments just because your income has increased. Wait to see if the rise is permanent and there are no other bills that take greater priority. You might have put off buying clothes for yourself or your children, or delayed essential repairs to your property. Get your life back together before you seek to make the banks happy. As long as your spending is sensible, the banks can wait, if that is what suits you.

Of course, if you can increase payments to cut the time you spend paying off debts, that must be good. The temptation with an informal arrangement will be the opposite – to approach creditors with a proposal to spread payments over a longer period of time. Unless your income has dropped dramatically, avoid doing this.

Creditors might agree to the plan, but it will leave you tied to a repayment for longer and delay the day when you get your life back on track (see the case study, overleaf).

❝ Never rush to increase payments because your income has increased. See if the rise is permanent and if there are higher priority bills. ❞

181

Case Study — Elizabeth Clark

Elizabeth Clark had negotiated an agreement with her creditors that she would pay three-quarters of her debts, which totalled £20,000. She also won an agreement for a freeze on interest and penalties, which meant that she needed to repay £15,000. The longer she takes to repay the debt, the smaller the monthly repayment would be:

Timescale (to repay £15,000)	Monthly payments
5 years	£250
7 years	£178
12 years	£104

A DEBT MANAGEMENT PLAN (DMP)

In many ways keeping to a DMP is simpler than an informal arrangement because it involves you paying one amount to a debt management company. The fee paid to the debt management adviser is part of the payment. The debt management business pays the creditors and keeps its fee.

You need to budget in just the same way as an informal arrangement and if your budgeting turns out to be unrealistic, you can go back to the adviser and ask for your payments to be reviewed.

AN INDIVIDUAL VOLUNTARY AGREEMENT (IVA)

An IVA is a legal contract and one of its aims is to reach a binding settlement that protects you from creditors seeking higher payments at a later stage. They must be satisfied with your offer and stick with it. The flipside of the agreement is that you must keep up your side of the bargain and maintain monthly payments. If you find that you can't continue to fund the payments, you will more than likely be pushed into bankruptcy as there is no scope for renegotiation with an IVA. You must therefore be even more stringent in your budgeting than if you have a DMP or informal arrangement.

“ There is no scope for renegotiation with an IVA so you must be stringent in your budgeting or you could face bankruptcy. ”

182

BANKRUPTCY

The official receiver can force you to accept an 'income payments agreement' for three years after the bankruptcy (see page 156). The agreement, which is imposed when creditors fail to recover an asset, comes as a shock to many people who think bankruptcy means that they have managed to leave their debts behind.

In answer to the request for an income payments agreement, you should reassess your income and outgoings again. Time will be short, so you won't be able to keep a cash diary, but the next best thing will be the piece of paper you used for your original budget. Take this with you to the official receiver having double-checked the figures to make sure they are up to date. You need to show the official receiver that you have no spare money to spend on debt repayments. The official receiver can take more than half of your disposable income for the three years the agreement can last.

If the official receiver presses ahead with the agreement, you should seek advice. Once an income payments agreement is in place, it is a legal contract and you must make every effort to pay the debt. If you don't, there will be further court proceedings.

WHAT IF YOU STILL SPEND?

Some people are so elated at gaining an agreement from creditors that they start spending freely all over again. Studies have shown that people who consolidate loans often fail to bring their income and spending back into line. Instead, they attempt to maintain the lifestyle they enjoy and start overspending.

To avoid building another debt mountain, here are some things you can do to help yourself:

- Stick to writing your cash diary.
- Cut up your credit cards and resist signing up for more.
- Tear up offers of loans through the post; they are only good for recycling.
- Open a basic bank account (see pages 187–90), which will prevent you taking out an overdraft.

If you cannot budget, ask friends and family to help you find a way to bring balance to your life and finances.

Giving up binge spending is like giving up smoking, except there is more help from doctors and the medical industry to help you quit cigarettes than an addiction to spending. While smoking is obviously more important because it will more than likely kill you, continuing to spend could jeopardise your house, your job and your relationships.

If you need to keep borrowing

There are many circumstances when you will need to borrow more money, even when you have just sorted out your debts. The general message is don't. If you have allowed debts to get out of control once, it can happen again. Why establish a routine that pulls you out of a debt spiral only to start the process all over again? Of course, there are times when this really can't be helped.

If the reason you got into trouble can be put down to divorce or separation, unemployment or a long illness, then while you might have pushed your worries to the back of your mind and hoped the financial consequences would go away, you are not necessarily the kind of person who ignores more routine debt problems.

There are different situations where you might need to take on more debt as part of your recovery plans. There is the person who is re-mortgaging and switching debts around for the best deal;

❝ There are a number of situations where you might need to take on more debt as part of your recovery plan. ❞

the person who allowed debts to get a bit out of control and consolidated their loans to make life simpler; the person who has found the only solution is an informal debt repayment plan, a formal debt management plan, or an IVA; and there is the person forced into bankruptcy.

THE RE-MORTGAGER

If you have re-mortgaged primarily to consolidate debts or to release funds for a particular project – a house extension, say, or a career change, a wedding or holiday – you must ask yourself is the extra debt necessary and how will you pay for it?

If your house price has appreciated since you last re-mortgaged, then another release of equity is the logical move to get your hands on a lump sum

 For more detailed information on re-mortgaging, see pages 101-5.

of cash, but there are pitfalls. A mortgage is not free money. Look at the calculations on page 95 and see if you can afford the repayments. Don't be tempted by the lure of an interest-only top-up to your existing mortgage. Or a mortgage that runs beyond the life of your current loan.

Most lenders will ask you to reduce mortgage debt at the same rate. So if a mortgage has already run for ten years and has 15 years left to run, the lender will be unwilling to offer a top-up mortgage loan to run for 20 years. Either you must pay the top-up loan over a 15-year period or move the main mortgage to 20 years.

Money management tip

Draw up a new domestic budget to check you can afford the new monthly payments. Use the monthly budget outline laid out on pages 22-5.

Paying both loans over 15 years will be more expensive to fund on a monthly basis, but extending the entire mortgage another five years to 20 years will mean you pay the lender much more than you ever envisaged in total interest. To illustrate the difference in cost between a 40-year mortgage and a 25-year mortgage, see the box on page 102.

The pros and cons of re-mortgaging

Pros	Cons
• You probably still have a good credit rating and will qualify for cheap loans. • Can be used to stabilise your finances and recover from unforeseen debt problems.	• Studies show more people than ever will be paying mortgages into retirement. You don't want to be one of them. Your income will almost certainly drop when you are over 65 years old and a mortgage will eat into what spare cash you have left. • Drawing out equity to pay for a holiday, wedding or another one-off event can be difficult to justify. Home improvements can be profitable in the long term, but further spending when you have only recently reached your limit cannot be justified. At this stage, if you cannot afford to save up to pay for the event, then you probably can't afford to repay a loan.

For many people, extending the term seems like the only thing to do, and if, like most people, you use the money drawn from your house to carry out essential repairs or modernise the interior, add a loft extension or extension to the back of your house, it could be a sensible decision.

> **“ If you are struggling to pay bills and thinking about taking a loan, you need to renegotiate your DMP as it is too generous to your creditors. ”**

WHEN YOU HAVE A DEBT MANAGEMENT PLAN (DMP)

A formal or informal DMP will severely limit your ability to source extra debt from mainstream lenders. When you approach such lenders for extra funds they will run a credit check and most likely refuse.

If they don't refuse, they will probably refer you to a subsidiary that lends to people with impaired credit records. This will be an opportunity for them to offer you a loan with extraordinarily high interest rates.

If you are struggling to pay bills and thinking about taking a loan, you are taking the wrong approach. Your finances are telling you to go back and renegotiate your DMP. It might be the more painful option (psychologically speaking), but if you cannot afford the repayments, then the original settlement was too generous to your creditors.

WHEN YOU HAVE AN INDIVIDUAL VOLUNTARY AGREEMENT (IVA)

There is no opportunity to renegotiate an IVA. Once the payments are agreed and the documents signed, you and your creditors are bound to a three-year deal.

Borrowing to solve cashflow problems or to pay outstanding bills should only be accompanied by big cuts in your

 If you can no long afford the repayments on a DMP, you might have no other choice but to become bankrupt rather than apply for an IVA - see pages 150 and 151-66.

outgoings to make sure it doesn't happen again. If you are a homeowner, you must declare to lenders that you are paying other creditors through an IVA.

" For every person who found bankruptcy a blessed relief, there is another who complains at their continuing problems dealing with lenders. **"**

WHEN YOU ARE A DISCHARGED BANKRUPT

It is easier than ever before to take out a mortgage and re-establish your life following a year as a bankrupt. But for every person who says bankruptcy was a blessed relief, there is another who complains that their problems dealing with banks and other lenders left them feeling abused and wishing they had never gone bust.

Once discharged, there are several lenders who will offer you a mortgage. But with house prices remaining high in most parts of the country, it will probably be a better bet renting a home to start with. It may at first seem cheaper to buy

a home, but hidden costs are rarely factored into the equation. House repairs, broken central heating boilers and boundary disputes with the neighbours are all someone else's problem when you rent.

If you do buy, there is the benefit of property price rises to make you feel richer. The feeling can disappear quite quickly, though, should the property become a millstone around your neck and the source of your next round of debt problems.

BASIC BANK ACCOUNTS

Basic bank accounts were a government idea to make high street banks cater for people on low incomes. They have developed in recent years into a safe haven for anyone who wants the services offered by a current account without the temptation of an overdraft facility.

It's a rare bank that advertises the benefits of basic banks accounts. In the main, banks don't like them because they think customers will be unlikely to buy their savings and investments or qualify for a loan, where they make lots of money. More enlightened banks, however, see them as a way to reach people who would otherwise be excluded from the banking system.

You can put your wages, benefits, tax credits and state pension into the account.

 For information on renting, see the *Which? Essential Guide Letting and Renting*.

The best accounts also offer standing orders and direct debits together with cash cards that behave like a debit card, using one of the mainstream money transfer systems, such as Visa or Switch/Maestro. These are the accounts you want. The main City regulator, the Financial Services Authority, has helpfully listed the main banks and building societies offering basic bank accounts and the facilities they offer (see box, opposite).

❝ The main drawback of a cash card is that you can't make use of good deals online, but you can upgrade after 6-12 months. ❞

Monthly direct debits/ standing orders

These allow you to budget more easily and are often a route to cheap deals. For instance, gas and electricity companies give you a discount if you combine your utilities and a further discount if you pay by direct debit.

Cash card

A cash card allows you to withdraw money and check your balance. To buy goods and services, other than those you pay for by direct debit, you must use cash. Check that you can withdraw at least £200 a day – some allow £300.

The main drawback is that you miss out on some of the cheapest goods and

services sold online. To buy goods online you need a card that connects through the Visa or Switch/Maestro networks. The Switch/Solo and Visa Electron brands, developed for basic bank accounts, are sometimes rejected by retailers and other online suppliers. If you can only register for an account with a Switch/Solo or Visa Electron, make sure you apply as quickly as possible for an upgrade to a standard card, usually after 6–12 months.

Mastercard will also work, but it is not used by banks to support basic bank accounts. Apart from credit cards, Mastercard only supports a selection of the pre-pay cards (see page 56).

Your credit rating will determine which card you get. If you are an undischarged bankrupt, you will find it difficult to get an account. Most banks allow discharged bankrupts.

The time to get a basic bank account is when you are heading for trouble. Your existing bank will probably be one of your creditors and will freeze cash in your current account. To pay bills and debts, set up your basic bank account at the earliest opportunity. Leave it until you have entered an IVA, DMP or bankruptcy and you could struggle to set one up.

Branches

You might have difficulty signing up with a bank that has a branch near you. Some banks have hooked up with the Post Office to offer more outlets, both to take in savings and withdraw cash. Basic bank account holders can tap into this extra network of branches, potentially saving

Using basic bank accounts

The best basic bank accounts will allow you to access them via:

- Branch
- Cash machine
- Digital TV
- Internet
- Post Office
- Postal service
- Telephone
- WAP/mobile phone.

But not all do. Many will exclude the internet and restrict you to the branch and telephone. Others are not members of the Post Office network with the result that the 14,000 Post Office branches are not open to you. So if you want to be able to use the Post Office as a means to pay in and withdraw money, choose from: Alliance & Leicester, Barclays (in England and Wales), cahoot, the Co-operative Bank, Lloyds TSB, smile and first direct (in Scotland only). It is always worth checking with your local branch of the Post Office if there are other banks available, too.

them a car journey or bus fare for each withdrawal when a bank branch is some distance away.

Unlike normal accounts, banks make sure chequebooks and overdraft facilities stay well out of reach of the basic bank account holder. In this way, you can only spend what is available in your account. However, you still need to keep an eye on your account balance if you have standing orders or direct debits set up. If there is not enough money in your account to pay these, they will be rejected and you will be charged.

Charges

The amount banks charge when you stray into overdraft varies widely. Some charge £15 a day, others £35 or even £38.50 in some cases. So check which offers the lowest before signing on the dotted line.

 For more information on tax credits, see pages 120–1. For more information and a comprehensive list of banks offering basic bank accounts see www.moneymadeclear.fsa.gov.uk/pdfs/bank_accounts.pdf.

There can be many reasons why you might drop into the red. If you can see it coming you should contact the bank and explain. One of the biggest problems in recent years has been the errors that plague tax credit awards and payments. If you receive payments late and incur charges, you must complain to the tax credit office and seek compensation.

If your tax credits are switched off in error, you might not have enough money in your account to honour other direct debits. In this instance, you must also contact the tax credit office. It can make emergency payments. If it resists your pleas, say you will claim compensation.

❝ One of the biggest problems in recent years has been errors in tax credit awards and payments. ❞

Consumer protection

A look back over recent decades shows us that finance companies spend most of their time developing products and then trying to sell them. Banks invent new kinds of current account; building societies want you to be seduced by their cashback fixed rate mortgage offer, and so it goes on.

Making a complaint

It takes lots of money to develop a new financial product, so once it is complete and ready to go, there is an almost desperate need on the part of the business to sell it to as many people as possible. Too often this situation has the painful effect of encouraging sales teams to persuade people to buy who don't need the product or can't afford it.

From pensions mis-selling through endowment mis-selling to payment protection insurance mis-selling, there are millions of people who have bought a financial product that was wrong for them. People who were mis-sold a personal pension, mostly in the early 1990s, had an easy ride when it came to compensation. For one thing, they didn't need to complain. The government said all pension companies must review their records and consider themselves guilty until proven innocent. Around 1.4 million people received compensation at a cost to the insurance industry of more than £11 billion.

The endowment scandal came next (see pages 106–9 for more on endowments). The regulator shifted its stance and said consumers must do all the hard work and complain to get redress. This decision had the effect, as you might imagine, of cutting down the amount paid in compensation. There was no doubt that millions of people would fail to pay off their home loan when the endowment they were told would do the job was a deeply flawed product. To stop them doing it again, there should be the same process as the one faced by the pensions industry. But endowments were sold by much the same companies and they battled for the regulator to be kinder to them.

A compromise meant that the companies that sold endowments – mainly banks and insurers and financial advisers – would only need to show that they explained the potential problems with endowments to their clients to escape paying compensation.

"Too often, the desire to make money encourages sales teams to persuade people who don't need (or can't afford) a product to buy it."

Responsible lending

Lenders have a duty to sell to consumers in a responsible way, but on many occasions have fallen short of standards agreed by the industry and monitored by their own trade body – the British Bankers Association. Some lenders have received a slap on the wrist, while others have been fined and reprimanded by the Financial Services Authority. All lenders will tell you it is not in their interests to get anything other than the best deal for their customers. However, there are thousands of finance companies wanting to lend money and the intense competition this generates puts pressure on the firms and their staff to sell more aggressively.

Banks and responsible lending

Most of the debate about bank lending has focused on how banks deal with people who have the highest debts in relation to their income. Debt advice agencies often deal with clients who have unsecured and secured loan debts worth five times their salary, excluding their mortgages.

Banks are under pressure from regulators to share information about their customers to prevent these situations arising. However, it will be some time before they can say with hand on heart that they have access to a full picture of each new customer before agreeing to a loan.

Which? and responsible lending

In 2006, Which? told a financial watchdog investigating responsible lending: 'The banks repeatedly claim that they lend responsibly by undertaking credit checks. Yet how can banks do this if they lack access to a complete picture of the applicant's existing debt burdens?' Banks say they abide by the rules as far as they can and it is other less reputable lenders that use the information available to target vulnerable customers and aggressively sell them more loans.

Read the small print

It is hard to know how much this is true. What it does show is that you need to tread carefully. It is a pain reading small print, but in these difficult times there is more important information in the small print than ever before.

Hold banks to account

If you think a lender has acted unfairly towards you, there are several channels for taking up a complaint. You can hold banks to account in a variety of ways. For more information on this subject see pages 194–5.

NEWER COMPLAINTS

At the moment, thousands of bank customers are complaining about bank charges that have, in some cases, added thousands of pounds to their debts. Another group of customers are just beginning to understand that the payment protection insurance (PPI) policy sold to them when they signed up for a credit card, personal loan or mortgage is, in most cases, an expensive waste of money. For more on the mis-selling of PPI see pages 56–9 and 197.

“ There is a confusing array of rights and responsibilities in the financial services arena. ”

Credit agreements

The OFT cannot provide advice or assistance to individual consumers or traders if they are having trouble with a credit agreement. If you need consumer advice, information on specific consumer rights or wish to make a consumer complaint, contact the Consumer Direct advice service on 08454 04 05 06 or visit the Consumer Direct website at www.consumerdirect.gov.uk.

FINANCIAL REGULATION

There is clearly a confusing array of rights and responsibilities for customers when they enter the financial services arena. The ultimate regulator, often known as the chief regulator or City watchdog, is the Financial Services Authority. It regulates lenders offering mortgages, credit card companies and areas of finance that can have an impact on debts like insurance.

Consumer protection issues are dealt with when complaints are made to the Director-General of Fair Trade. The Office of Fair Trading (OFT) will then investigate, impose an injunction or take the matter to litigation. The OFT also acts as the UK's official consumer and competition watchdog, with a remit to make markets work well for consumers, and at a local, municipal level, by Trading Standards departments.

BANKING CODES OF CONDUCT

The Banking Code Standards Board (BCSB) is the self-regulating body that oversees the behaviour of Britain's banks and credit card companies. It polices the banks' voluntary codes of practice. In the event of a dispute between a bank and a customer that cannot be resolved by either the bank or the standards board, then the Financial Ombudsman Service (FOS) steps into the fray.

 To find out more about the Financial Services Authority, go to www.fsa.gov.uk and for the Office of Fair Trading, go to www.oft.gov.uk.

The Banking Code Standards Board

The BCSB polices the banking code, which governs the behaviour of banks towards their customers. The Banking Code sets minimum standards for the way in which banks, building societies and other banking service providers treat their customers. Copies of the Banking Code can be obtained from any high street bank or building society or via your card issuer (see also the box, below).

The BCSB has a compliance policy that sets out its powers. It says that one of the most effective is that of public censure – the ability to 'name and shame' banks, building societies or card issuers that have been found guilty of a material breach. It says: 'We also have the ability to issue "directions as to future conduct" or to recommend compensation for past breaches, normally where a group of customers has been disadvantaged. Examples of how we have exercised these powers in the past are available on our website.'

The Code covers a multitude of financial products, including personal loans and overdrafts, card products, mortgages and general insurance where they are sold by banks. The BCSB will act on your complaints against the bank and on tip-offs by whistle-blowers warning of their bad behaviour. But first you must write to your bank spelling out your complaint.

Within four weeks, they must write back with a final response or explain to you why they need more time to resolve your complaint. By eight weeks they must send you their final response.

The Financial Ombudsman Services

If you fail to resolve your dispute with a bank through the BCSB, you can take the case to the FOS. The FOS has spent recent years battling to cope with a mountain of disputes between consumers and the financial services industry. In 2007, its workload is expected to be the largest ever with endowment mortgages and bank charges the two most popular complaints.

It was set up to help settle disputes between individuals or small businesses and financial firms. The service is free to consumers. The FOS's decisions are binding on firms and it can make awards of up to £100,000. The FOS takes account of the Banking Code in reaching its decision, as well as banking law and practice. If it feels that the Code has been broken, it may inform the BCSB, so that further action can be taken. For more information, see the FOS leaflet 'Your Complaint and the Ombudsman' and its website www.financial-ombudsman.org.uk.

 The Banking Code is also available online at www.bankingcode.org.uk. The website also outlines how you can make complaints about financial institutions.

Mis-selling and over charging

A finance company has a duty of care and the care it takes is addressed to different audiences. Customers are important and the company will usually need to satisfy guidelines covering its sales and marketing, especially lenders. It will need to satisfy regulations set down by the regulator, most often the Financial Services Authority.

HOW TO COMPLAIN

You might be in debt because you were mis-sold a loan with high charges you could never afford. The loan might have been sold with protection insurance that added to your debts bills. Your situation might have forced you into overdraft and sparked a flurry of fees and charges that were unfair and made your debts spiral.

If you believe it is possible that a bank or other finance company sold you a product that you didn't need or couldn't afford, you may have grounds for a complaint. Thousands of people have complained about being mis-sold protection insurance and hundreds of thousands of people have complained about bank charges. Mis-selling is common and the only way it is going to stop is if everyone affected complains and punishes the companies involved by demanding compensation.

If you were mis-sold a personal loan

Loans are covered by the Consumer Credit Act. If you believe you were misled when sold a loan, either unsecured or secured, you can complain to the OFT. It will either deal with the complaint itself or give the job to your local trading standards officers.

❝Huge numbers of people have complained about protection insurance and bank charges.❞

 The website for the Financial Ombudsman Service is www.financial-ombudsman.org.uk where there are quick links to the most common complaints procedures.

If you were mis-sold payment protection insurance (PPI)

Under guidelines for selling general insurance products, providers are supposed to explain how PPI works and what it costs. The costs should be spelled out separately to the costs of the loan. Complaints should be made to the Financial Ombudsman Service if you cannot get any satisfaction from the organisation that sold you the PPI policy.

If you were unfairly charged penalty fees

Thousands of bank customers have reclaimed penalty fees after a long campaign to highlight that the unfair nature of the charges means they are legally indefensible. A survey in 2006 found that one in four of us had used an unauthorised overdraft in the previous year. While banks are providing a service to consumers who go into unauthorised overdraft, Which? says they are 'also raking in the cash – to the tune of an astonishing £4.7 billion in the last year' (as of June 2006). Banks have needed to set aside millions of pounds to compensate customers who were charged penalty fees and in many cases plunged into debt as a result.

Which? has led the campaign against excessive bank charges and has produced a step-by-step guide to help you get your money back (see right). According to Which?, bank charges are a breach of consumer contract regulations. The Unfair Terms in Consumer Contract Regulations (1999) state that charges can only cover the costs the bank incurs. These charges cannot be used as a deterrent or a profit stream by the bank. Which? thinks bank charges are therefore disproportionate to the amount it actually costs the bank to deal with an account in the red. Some critics have called on the banks to open their books and justify their charges – something they haven't done so far.

❝ A long campaign highlighted the fact that these unfair charges are legally indefensible. ❞

KEY STEPS TO COMPLAINING ABOUT BANK CHARGES

To complain, follow these steps and also use Which?'s bank charges template letters (see pages 200–4). More than 300,000 template letters have already been downloaded from Which?'s website and people are successfully reclaiming their money from the banks. If you get little or no satisfaction, you can then complain to the Financial Ombudsman Service.

Step 1: avoid being charged

The easiest way to avoid being charged for slipping into an unauthorised overdraft is to contact your bank immediately if you think you may have become overdrawn or exceeded your arranged overdraft. Contact your bank and explain your situation. They may agree to offer you a larger overdraft facility.

Step 2: work out how much you've paid

By law, you can make a claim for charges paid on unauthorised overdrafts in the last six years. Unless you have kept all your bank statements for this time, you will need to write to your bank and ask them to provide this information. Use Letter One 'How much have I paid?' on page 201 as a template.

Under the Data Protection Act 1998, the company must provide this information within 40 days and they cannot charge more than £10 for doing so. Note that the company may try to charge you more for providing copy statements (this charge is usually explained on the back of statements), but if you request a computer printout of charges, which is acceptable evidence, they cannot charge more than £10. Do not be put off by an attempt by a company to prevent you getting your right to information. If you experience problems contact the Information Commissioner (see box, below).

❝ Do not be put off by an attempt to prevent you getting the information you have a right to see. ❞

Step 3: complain to your bank or building society

Write to your bank, telling them that you are unhappy with the charges you have paid as you believe they have breached regulations. Go on to detail the total amount of charges you are complaining about and seek a refund from them. Use Letter Two 'Complain to your bank' on page 203 as a template.

The bank has a maximum of eight weeks to respond and resolve your complaint. They should respond within four weeks, but they must resolve the complaint within eight weeks or allow you to go straight to the Financial Ombudsman Service. The rules over how long a bank should take to resolve your complaint are set out by their regulator, the Financial Services Authority (www.fsa.gov.uk).

Your bank may agree to pay back all or some of your money. A Which? survey in March 2007 found that 85 per cent of people who had challenged bank charges had received a full or partial refund. We think the figure would be closer to 100 per cent if people took their case further to the Financial Ombudsman Service or the small claims court, although the latter should only be used as a last resort (see Step 5). To date, banks appear to be settling cases.

 The Information Commissioner's Office is the UK's independent authority set up to promote access to official information and to protect personal information. Its website address is www.ico.gov.uk.

Step 4: take your case to the Financial Ombudsman Service

If your bank refuses to refund any of your charges, or they make you an offer you are not happy with, you can refer them to the Financial Ombudsman Service (FOS). FOS is a free and independent service that helps settle disputes between financial services business and consumers. They step in when a firm and consumer cannot settle a complaint, in this case, if your bank will not refund all or some of your unfair bank charges. You need to have first taken your complaint to your bank before approaching FOS.

You can refer your case to FOS if:

- **Eight weeks has passed** from when you sent your complaint into your bank, OR
- **Your bank has sent you a letter** saying their charges are fair, OR
- **Your bank has made you an offer to partially refund** your charges, but you aren't happy with their offer, OR
- **Your bank is threatening to close your account down** if you challenge charges, OR
- **You're not happy** with the way your bank has been treating you.

You will need to fill in the FOS complaint form and send supporting documents, such as your letter and the response from your bank, to the Ombudsman. This will help them understand what exactly your complaint is about. FOS can help fill in the form over the phone.

There is no fee or charge to take your complaint to FOS, and you will not be liable for the firm's legal costs, even if your complaint isn't upheld. So far, banks have chosen to settle all cases referred by consumers to the Ombudsman.

If the Ombudsman doesn't uphold your complaint, you can still take legal action, although a judge may take into consideration the FOS's decision. Legal action can also be costly and time consuming.

Step 5: take your case to the small claims court

Another alternative to FOS for reclaiming unfair charges is to take your bank to the small claims court. The small claims court is relatively easy to use, but before proceeding, see the information on the Which? website (www.which.co.uk), which outlines how the process works.

❝ An alternative is to take your bank to the small claims court. ❞

For more information about taking your case to the small claims court, see the *Which? Essential Guide Making a Civil Claim.*

Bank charges Letter One: How much have I paid?

- This letter asks your bank to send you a list of all the default charges (on unauthorised overdrafts and unpaid direct debits) applied to your account in the last six years. You only need to send this if you want your money back and have not kept bank statements. You can ignore this letter and go straight to Letter Two if you already have details of all the default charges you have paid.

- Your bank may decide not to send you a list of the charges, but instead send you copies of six years' worth of statements. You will then need to go through and make a note of all the charges.

- The bank must supply this information under the Data Protection Act 1998. If your bank makes a charge for this information, the charge cannot be more than £10.

- Check carefully through the template text opposite and insert your personal information where indicated in square brackets.

❝ Your bank may decide not to send you a list of charges, but instead supply six years' worth of statements. ❞

❝ To download sample letters, go to www.which.co.uk/money. ❞

[INSERT YOUR HOME ADDRESS]

[INSERT TODAY'S DATE]

[INSERT THE NAME OF YOUR BANK]

[INSERT THE ADDRESS OF YOUR BANK]

Re: Account number [INSERT YOUR ACCOUNT NUMBER]

Dear Sir/Madam

I request that [INSERT THE NAME OF YOUR BANK] provides me with details of all default charges for unauthorised overdrafts and unpaid direct debits and standing orders I have paid in the last six years.

I understand that [INSERT THE NAME OF YOUR BANK] is obliged to provide this information under the Data Protection Act 1998.

I look forward to hearing from you within 40 days.

Yours faithfully

[SIGN YOUR NAME]

[TYPE YOUR NAME]

Bank charges Letter Two:
Complain to your bank

- This letter tells your bank that you are unhappy with default charges (on unauthorised overdrafts and unpaid direct debits) you have paid in the last six years and you are asking for them to be refunded, or you will take your case to the Financial Ombudsman Service.

- Check through carefully and insert your personal information where indicated in square brackets. The fifth paragraph (beginning 'I am only prepared...') is very important if you are claiming charges. It shows that you are acting reasonably.

- If your bank still refuses to pay back your money, the Financial Ombudsman Service is the next step.

❝To download sample letters, go to www.which.co.uk/money.❞

❝If your bank refused to pay back your money, the next step is the Financial Ombudsman Services.❞

[INSERT YOUR HOME ADDRESS]

[INSERT TODAY'S DATE]

[INSERT THE NAME OF YOUR BANK]

[INSERT THE ADDRESS OF YOUR BANK]

Re: Default charges on account number [INSERT YOUR ACCOUNT NUMBER]

Dear Sir/Madam

I refer to default charges relating to unauthorised overdrafts which have been applied to my account by [INSERT THE NAME OF YOUR BANK], amounting to [INSERT THE FULL AMOUNT OF THE BANK CHARGES].

The basis for this request is under the Unfair Terms in Consumer Contract Regulations and/or the law of penalties. The bank charges applied to my account are unfair under schedule 2(e) of the Unfair Terms in Consumer Contracts Regulations 1999 (the regulations), which states that *a term is unfair if it requires any consumer who fails to fulfil his/her obligation to pay a disproportionately high sum in compensation*. In this instance [INSERT THE NAME OF YOUR BANK] has charged me an amount which is not proportionate to the amount borrowed.

The amount charged by [INSERT THE NAME OF YOUR BANK] is a penalty charge, which, under the law of penalties, is 'extravagant' and therefore unlawful.

I am only prepared to pay the charges on condition that the bank agrees to repay me the full amount, if the Financial Ombudsman Service finds in my favour and declares the charges unenforceable.

I therefore ask that you repay the amount of all these charges, [INSERT THE FULL AMOUNT OF THE BANK CHARGES].

I look forward to receiving your response within a maximum of eight weeks of the date of this letter or I will issue proceedings with the Financial Ombudsman Service to reclaim the full amount of charges.

I am happy for you to contact me on [INSERT YOUR TELEPHONE NUMBER] to discuss the matter.

Yours faithfully

[SIGN YOUR NAME]

[TYPE YOUR NAME]

Glossary

Affidavit: A sworn witness statement.

Annual equivalent rate (AER): This figure appears as a percentage and illustrates what the interest rate would be if the interest was added to your account once each year. It is usually applied to savings and excludes any bonus interest that may be payable.

Annual percentage rate (APR): The APR is the average interest rate paid over the term of the loan/mortgage including any discounts and fees.

Available credit: The difference between the amount you have spent on a credit or debit card and the credit limit, which is how much you have left to spend on the card.

Bailiff: A person licensed to confiscate your property to pay a debt. Bailiffs must have documents confirming their identity and that a court has sanctioned them to retrieve goods on behalf of one of your creditors. There are complicated rules about what they can take and how they can take it. If one appears at your door, refuse him or her entry and seek advice immediately.

Balance transfer: The borrowings transferred from one credit card to another. Card companies often advertise an interest-free term of up to a year or 18 months to encourage you to switch your debt to their card, but will charge up to 3 per cent of the balance as a fee.

Bank of England: The Bank's monetary policy committee sets interest base rates to meet the government's inflation target. Base rate changes are a strong guide to changes in mortgage rates.

Bankrupt: When you become insolvent and have no money to pay creditors, you may find the best course of action is to become bankrupt. It is a legal process that protects you from further claims by creditors. You can emerge from bankruptcy in one year or sometimes less, but all your main assets will be sold to pay debts.

Bankruptcy petition: An application to the county court for bankruptcy proceedings to start. Can be requested by either a debtor wishing to make him- or herself bankrupt or a creditor pursuing a debtor.

Bankruptcy restriction order (or undertaking): Additional restrictions on bankrupts whose conduct is considered to have been dishonest or blameworthy.

Bridging loan: A type of loan that can be taken out by people moving house who want to move into their new home before selling their old one. Banks charge high rates of interest, which can be crippling if the old house fails to sell quickly.

Broker: The term used to describe an intermediary between a buyer and a seller. Mortgage brokers, insurance brokers and stockbrokers are all covered by the term. Some of these intermediaries may call themselves 'agents' or 'consultants', but they all perform a similar job. Some brokers are tied to offering deals from a limited pool of suppliers, others are not. They are obliged to tell you either way.

Buildings insurance: Policies that cover the cost of repairs if your property is damaged or destroyed.

Building society: These differ from banks in that they are owned by members rather than shareholders. Any surpluses are supposed to be distributed to members in the form of lower interest rates on mortgages and higher interest rates on savings.

Buy-to-let mortgage: A mortgage that allows landlords to buy a property that they can let to tenants. Landlords will usually need a deposit, often around 20 per cent, and pay a higher interest rate than homebuyers. They must also show the rent on the property will more than cover mortgage repayments.

Capped-rate mortgage: A half-way house between variable rate and fixed rate mortgages. Interest rates rise and fall in line with the lender's standard variable rate, but are 'capped' so that they cannot exceed a certain level. This means you can benefit from falls in interest rates but

are protected from increases above a certain limit.

Cash annual rate: A term used by credit card companies. Always higher than the balance transfer or purchase rates, it usually refers to a punishing interest rate that applies to cash withdrawals using the card or cheques supplied by the card company.

Cash limit: The amount a bank or credit card company will allow you to withdraw in cash using their card.

Certificated bailiff: Allowed to seize goods for the widest range of creditors, including councils for unpaid council tax, traffic offences and unpaid rent.

Charging order: A charging order is placed by the court on a debtor's property, usually his or her home, for money owed to a lender. If you have a personal loan and you have not kept to the repayment arrangement, a lender can request the court to place a charging order on your property so that when the property is sold you will have to pay that debt before any of the proceeds are given to you.

Civil court: The High Court in London and county courts around the country hear civil cases. You won't have committed a criminal act by reneging on debts, so cases are not heard in magistrate or crown courts. A judge will hear the case, though most are uncontested and a formality. There are costs applied by the court that can be waived if you are on a low income.

Consolidated loans: If you have multiple debts with different lenders – on credit cards, loans, with friends and family – you can shift them all to a single loan, also known as a debt consolidation loan. You can consolidate debts in a personal loan or an unsecured loan.

County court judgement: A judgement for a debt by the county court. Creditors must get a county court judgement before they can instruct bailiffs to seize your possessions.

Credit card: Credit cards provide one of the easiest means of borrowing over a short period. You can use them to buy goods and withdraw cash, then pay back in full or in part at the end of the month. There is usually a minimum monthly payment of £5, or 5 per cent of the outstanding balance on your card, or the entire balance if it is less than £5 – whichever is greater.

Credit limit: The amount of money you can spend on the card. Put another way, it is the total amount you can borrow. The limit is set by the card company and will mainly depend on your credit score, income and employment.

Credit reference agency: When you apply for credit, the lender uses credit reference agencies to check your credit report. The agencies hold information on just about every adult in the UK, covering bank accounts, loans, mortgages, any previous credit agreements. Also reports of defaults on repayments and other people connected with your home address. Everyone has the right to see their own record held by the agencies.

Credit report: Your credit history is held on several credit reference agency

databases and credit card companies and banks look at your credit history and give you a report. Each company uses its own scoring method.

Critical illness cover: An insurance policy that pays out a tax-free lump sum if you are diagnosed with one of a list of diseases.

Default notice: A form sent by creditors, but this is a legal procedure to protect lenders and not something to worry about. The default notice must allow you at least seven days to comply with the action required. It doesn't necessarily mean the creditor intends to take you to court, especially if you pay the bill.

Dividend: An annual payment made by companies out of their profits to their shareholders. It repays the investment made by shareholders in the company.

Enforcement agent: Another name for a bailiff.

Endowment policy: Endowments are investment schemes that include life assurance. Most were sold with mortgages. You paid a monthly premium to an insurer and the policy was intended to grow to a value sufficient to repay your home loan and, possibly, produce a surplus lump sum as well. Most 25-year policies sold in the 1990s, and some sold earlier, are expected to miss their target.

Equity: Your share of an asset. If you buy shares in a company, you are said to have equity in the business. Equity is also referred to as the proportion of your home that you own, over and above a mortgage.

Equity release scheme: Sold by insurance companies, banks and building societies to mainly retired homeowners who retain the right to stay in the property for the rest of their life. One type of scheme involves you selling a portion of your home in return for a cash lump sum. When you die, the part of the property you sold will belong to the reversion company. The other type of scheme is a mortgage that releases cash, with the mortgage payments deducted from the house value when you die.

Financial Services Authority (FSA): The FSA regulates almost every type of financial services firm. It regulates banks, building societies, credit unions, insurance and investment firms (stockbrokers and fund managers) and independent financial advisers. It has powers to investigate, discipline and prosecute. If you want to make a complaint or get advice, visit the FSA's website: www.fsa.gov.uk.

Fixed-rate mortgage: A mortgage where the interest you pay, and therefore your monthly repayments, remains the same for an agreed period.

Flexible mortgage: Flexible mortgages allow you to make extra lump sum or monthly payments, borrow back money, take payment holidays and make underpayments. Most mortgages allow some flexibility, but you will pay a higher interest rate if you want to treat your mortgage like a bank account.

Freehold: A freehold gives the purchaser outright ownership of their home and the land it sits on. A freeholder has the right to do as they like with their home and garden, subject to the law and planning controls. *See also Leasehold.*

Housing Benefit: If you rent accommodation and are on a low income, you can qualify for help with the payments from your local council.

Income payments agreement: The official receiver or trustee in bankruptcy can ask you to agree to make regular payments to your creditors for three years from your income. It can demand more than half your disposable income.

Income payments order: If you fail to agree an income payment after bankruptcy, the official receiver can order you to pay and tell your employer to deduct the money from your salary.

Income protection insurance: Also known as long-term disability insurance, this pays a monthly amount if you are unable to work because of an illness or disability. The most you can insure is usually 60 per cent of your gross income, but you can use it to pay whichever bills are most important.

Income Support: A benefit that provides financial help for people between 16 and 60 who are on a low income and not in full-time paid work and not claiming other benefits. It is not paid to unemployed people actively seeking work (they can claim Jobseeker's Allowance).

Income Support for Mortgage Interest (ISMI): This benefit is paid to homeowners who are made redundant, unemployed or ill, but only after nine months.

Independent financial adviser (IFA): An IFA should give you advice about your finances and choose financial products from the full range on offer. They work on the basis of fees or commission. If you agree to commission payments, the companies from which you buy financial products pay the IFA.

Individual voluntary arrangement (IVA): A form of insolvency that stops short of bankruptcy. It is a legal contract between you and your creditors that allows you to pay them all or some of the debt owed. You must stick to the agreed monthly payments for five years while your creditors must agree not to harass you for more than the sum originally agreed. After the five years you are clear to borrow again.

Insolvency: This is the catch-all phrase for someone who cannot pay their debts and cannot agree an informal repayment plan with their creditors. There are two main routes for the insolvent person to take – both are forms of bankruptcy and have been established by the government as legal contracts that the debtor and creditor must abide by.

Insolvency practitioner: An authorised person who specialises in insolvency, usually an accountant or solicitor. They are authorised either by the Insolvency Service or by one of a number of recognised professional bodies.

Insolvency Service: Government agency that advises on insolvency, regulates the insolvency industry and oversees the official receiver.

Interest-only mortgage: A home loan where your monthly payments only go towards paying off the interest. You would normally set up a separate investment alongside to pay the capital sum when you reach the end of the mortgage term.

Jobcentre Plus: The government-run chain of offices that deal with job hunting and benefit claims. For information about your local branch, visit the Department of Work and Pensions' website: www.dwp.gov.uk.

Jobseeker's Allowance: A benefit that may be claimed by people who are available for and actively seeking work. To apply, visit a Jobcentre Plus office. They might make you claim with your partner.

Leasehold: A leasehold property is leased from the freeholder for a specified period of time. Leases specify the leaseholders' responsibilities to the property and the payments for the upkeep, which can be considerable.

Liability: Any legally enforceable obligation.

Life insurance: If you die, this insurance cover will pay a lump sum to your partner or whoever inherits your estate. If you are the main wage earner and don't have life insurance, your partner could be left to pay a mortgage and other bills on a low income. Always check if life insurance is paid via your pension, if you have one.

Lifetime balances: Several card companies will offer a balance transfer that attracts a low rate until it is paid in full. It may be 4.9 per cent or 5.9 per cent rather than the 0 per cent offered for a fixed period.

Liquid asset: An asset that can be converted easily into cash.

Loan-to-value (LTV): The ratio between the size of a mortgage and the valuation of the property. For instance, a loan-to-value of 90 per cent would mean borrowing £90,000 to buy a £100,000 home.

Minimum payment: The amount you must pay each month on a credit card to avoid a penalty charge of (maximum) £12. It is usually around 2 per cent of the balance, so a £5,000 balance will have a minimum payment of £100 a month.

Monthly repayment: The amount you decide to pay to reduce your credit card balance. It can be sent to the card company as a cheque, paid in at a bank branch or by direct debit.

Mortgage broker: An intermediary who offers advice on choosing a mortgage and helps you compare deals from different lenders.

Mortgage indemnity protection/ guarantee (MIP or MIG): Mortgage lenders can charge a one-off fee, often amounting to several thousand pounds, in the form of mortgage indemnity protection or guarantee when you buy a home. It protects

the lender against a fall in the home's value when you only have a small deposit and high loan-to-value. It should be avoided. This insurance policy protects your lender, yet it's you, the borrower, who pays the premium.

Mortgage term: The period over which you agree to repay your mortgage. This is typically 25 years, but increasingly lenders offer more flexible terms up to 40 years.

Mutuality: Some businesses are owned by their members (*See also Building societies*). These mutual organisations are supposed to give their profits back to members in the form of cheaper products.

National insurance contributions (NICs): National insurance is a form of tax that everyone in work must pay in order to qualify for benefits, including the state pension.

Negative equity: If the value of your property falls below the amount of the loan taken out to buy it, you are said to have negative equity. You are paying for something that is worth less than you paid for it.

Official receiver: An officer of the court and civil servant employed by the Insolvency Service who deals with bankruptcies and compulsory company liquidations.

Overdraft: An expensive form of borrowing using your current account. Banks typically allow customers an agreed overdraft limit that charges interest. Beyond the limit it will charge interest and penalty charges.

Payment holiday: A lender can allow you to miss a payment for a month or sometimes several months. This is known as a payment holiday. Lenders offering personal loans and secured loans can agree to a payment holiday, but usually make extra charges.

Payment protection policies: Insurance policy designed to cover payments on credit cards, loans and mortgages. Huge drawbacks with these policies are rarely mentioned by lenders who make vast profits selling them. If you really need to cover your payments, opt for an income protection plan sold by an independent broker.

Personal loan: A fixed amount of money borrowed from a bank or other lender. Usually unsecured (see below) and can be used to pay for things such as holidays, cars and weddings. Can also be used to consolidate other debts from credit cards and other loans (not mortgages). The usual term of the loan is three or five years. The maximum is ten years.

Provider: A credit card company.

Purchase annual rate: Like the balance transfer rate, it can be offered at '0 per cent' before reverting to a higher rate once the offer period has expired.

Repayment mortgage: A home loan where your monthly payments go towards paying off both the interest and the capital you borrowed. *See also Interest-only mortgage.*

Secured loan: A fixed amount of money borrowed from a specialist lender. The loan guarantees the lender it will get its money back if you can no longer afford the payments. Usually your home will be used as security for the loan. If you already have a mortgage, it will be the equivalent of a second mortgage. The usual term of the loan is 10–25 years.

Self-certification mortgage: Allows a homebuyer to verify his or her own income when applying for a mortgage. Usually the homebuyer will be self-employed or have an irregular income. The mortgages tend to come with higher interest rates than other standard home loans. The FSA is concerned that lenders allow homebuyers to exaggerate their incomes and put their mortgage repayments at risk.

Shareholders: People who own a share in a limited company; can also be institutions such as pension funds.

Stamp duty: A tax paid on share dealing of 0.5 per cent. Stamp duty is also the name given to a tax paid on house buying. You pay 1 per cent duty on properties worth between £130,000 and £250,000, 3 per cent on those worth between £250,000 and £500,000, and 4 per cent on properties worth £500,000 and over.

Standard variable rate (SVR): The rate charged for mortgages that are NOT on a special deal. Introductory mortgage offers revert to the SVR when they come to the end of the offer period.

Standing order: An instruction to the bank by the account holder to pay an agreed sum of money to another account. It is more flexible than a direct debit and must be renewed after a certain period, unlike a direct debit.

Statement of affairs: A form sent by the court asking you to give details about your financial situation and the reasons for the bankruptcy.

Summons: A call to attend a court hearing.

Tax year: The 12 months starting from 6 April in one year and ending with 5 April in the next.

Term assurance: A form of life insurance that covers an agreed term. Usually only needed when you have dependents. It pays a lump sum if you die within a specified period – for example, 10 years or 25 years.

Traded endowment policy: These policies allow you to sell your endowment rather than cash it in. Can offer better value, but should be assessed by a financial adviser to see if a sale is the best route.

Uncertificated bailiff: More likely to be used by courts to pursue basic credit debts.

Unsecured loan: A loan offered without security. It is a contractual arrangement in which you agree to repay the loan. Lenders will make a judgement based on your credit rating and employment status and income. Usually a fixed interest rate applies. Such loans are commonly paid back over three or five years.

Walking possession agreement: The bailiff can agree to a payment plan and leave the goods he or she wants to seize, this is called walking possession. Usually you will promise to pay some of your debt in return for keeping your possessions, though any breach will allow the bailiff to use the walking possession agreement to seize goods.

Winding-up order: Order of a court, usually based on a creditor's petition, for the compulsory winding-up or liquidation of a company or partnership.

Glossary

Useful addresses

Association of British Credit Unions
Holyoake House
Hanover Street
Manchester M60
Tel: 0161 832 3694
www.abcul.org

Association of Civil Enforcement Agencies
Chesham House
150 Regent Street
London W1R 5FA
Tel: 020 7432 0366
www.acea.org.uk

Banking Code Standards Board
Level 12, City Tower
40 Basinghall Street
London EC2V 5DE
Tel: 0845 230 9694
www.bankingcode.org.uk

Bankruptcy Advisory Service
2 Greenways
Swanland Hill
North Ferriby
Hull HU14 3JN
Tel: 01482 633034/5
www.bankruptcyadvisoryservice.co.uk

The Bankruptcy Association
FREEPOST LA1118
4 Johnson Close
LANCASTER
LA1 5BR
Tel: 01524 782713
www.theba.org.uk

Call Credit
Consumer Service Department
Park Row House
Leeds LS1 5JF
Tel: 0870 060 1414
www.callcredit.co.uk

CIFAS
4th Floor
Central House
14 Upper Woburn Place
London WC1H 0NN
Tel: c/o Equifax on 0870 010 2091
(Mon–Fri, 8am–6pm)
www.cifas.org.uk

Citizens Advice Bureau
For your nearest office, look in your local
phone book or go to
www.adviceguide.org.uk

**Consumer Credit Counselling Service
(CCCS)**
Wade House
Merrion Centre
Leeds LS 2 8NG
Tel: 0800 138 1111
www.cccs.co.uk

Consumer Direct
Advice line: 08454 04 05 06
www.consumerdirect.gov.uk

Child Support Agency
National Helpline
PO Box 55
Brierly Hill DY5 1YL
Tel: 08457 133 133 (Mon–Fri,
8am–8pm; Sat, 9am–5pm)
www.csa.gov.uk

Credit Action
Howard House
The Point
Weaver Road
Lincoln LN6 3QN
Tel: 0207 436 9937
www.creditaction.org.uk

Enforcement Services Association
Park House
10 Park Street
Bristol BS1 5HX
Tel: 0117 907 4771
www.ensas.org.uk

Equifax
Credit File Advice Centre
PO Box 1140
Bradford BD1 5US
Tel: 0845 600 1772
www.equifax.co.uk

Experian
The Consumer Help Service
PO Box 8000
Nottingham NG1 5GX
Tel: 0870 2416212
www.experian.co.uk

Financial Ombudsman Service
South Quay Plaza
183 Marsh Wall
London E14 9SR
Tel: 0845 080 1800
www.financial-ombudsman.org.uk

Financial Services Authority (FSA)
25 The North Colonnade
Canary Wharf
London E14 5HS
Consumer helpline: 0845 606 1234
www.fsa.gov.uk
also www.moneymadeclear.fsa.gov.uk

Help the Aged
207–221 Pentonville Road
London N1 9UZ
Tel: 0808 800 6565
www.helptheaged.org.uk

HM Courts Service
Customer Service Unit
5th Floor
Clive House
Petty France
London SW1H 9EX
Tel: 020 7189 2000 or 0845 456 8770
www.hmcourts-service.gov.uk

HM Revenue & Customs
Somerset House
Strand
London WC2R 1LB
Tel: 0845 302 1444 (Child Benefit)
Tel: 0845 302 1479 (National Insurance
Contributions)
Tel: 0845 900 0444 (self-assessment/
income tax)
Tel: 0845 300 3900 (Tax Credits)
www.hmrc.gov.uk

Office of Fair Trading
Fleetbank House
2–6 Salisbury Square
London EC4Y 8JX
Tel: 08457 22 44 99
www.oft.gov.uk

213

IFA Promotion
117 Farringdon Rd
London EC1R 3BX
Tel: 020 7833 3131
Consumer hotline: 0800 085 3250
www.impartial.co.uk

Information Commissioner's Office
Wycliffe House
Water Lane
Wilmslow SK9 5AF
Tel: 01625 545 745
www.ico.gov.uk

Insolvency Service
21 Bloomsbury Street
London WC1B 3QW
Insolvency helpline: 0845 602 9848
www.insolvency.gov.uk

Ministry of Justice
Selborne House
54 Victoria Street
London SW1E 6QW
Tel: 020 7210 8500
www.justice.gov.uk

National Association of Investigators and Process Servers
C/o Peace of Mind Investigations
33 Greenville Drive
Low Moor
Bradford BD12 0PT
Tel: 0845 1260759.
www.naips.co.uk

National Debtline
The Arch
48–52 Fllodgate Street
Birmingham B5 5SL
Tel: 0808 808 4000
www.nationadebtline.co.uk

Payplan
Kempton House
Dysart Road
Grantham
LincolnshireNG31 7LE
Tel: 0800 917 7823
www.payplan.com

The Pension Service
Tel: 0845 60 60 265 (Mon–Fri, 8am–8pm)
www.pensions.gov.uk

Pensions Advisory Service (OPAS)
11 Belgrave Road
London SW1V 1RB
Tel: 0845 601 2923
www.opas.org.uk

Redundancy Payments Office
Customer Service Unit
7th Floor
83–85 Hagley House
Birmingham B16 8QG
Tel: 0845 145 0004
www.redundancyhelp.co.uk

Student Loans Company
Customer Assistance Team
100 Bothwell Street
Glasgow G2 7JD
Tel: 08456 077 577
www.slc.co.uk

TaxAid
Room 304
Linton House
164–180 Union Street
London SE1 0LH
Tel: 0845 120 3779 (Mon–Thurs, 10am–12 noon)
www.taxaid.org.uk

Index

Index

which?

Which? Books

Other books in this series

The Tax Handbook 2007/8

Tony Levene
ISBN: 978 1 84490 039 8
Price £10.99

Make sense of the complicated rules, legislation and red-tape with *The Tax Handbook 2007/8*. Written by Guardian finance journalist and tax expert Tony Levene, this essential guide gives expert advice on all aspects of the UK tax system and does the footwork for you. It includes information on finding the right accountant and how to get the best from them, advice on NI contributions, tax credits for families and the self-assessment form. An indispensable guide for anyone who pays tax.

Working for Yourself

Mike Pywell and Bill Hilton
ISBN: 978 1 84490 040 4
Price £10.99

Working for Yourself is a practical and straightforward guide, aimed at people who are planning the jump from a salaried, permanent contract to a freelance/entrepreneurial lifestyle. Pointing out the benefits and prospective pitfalls of being self-employed, this essential guide then details pertinent financial and legal information, as well as suggesting when and where to seek professional help.

Making a Civil Claim

Melanie McDonald
ISBN: 978 1 84490 037 4
Price £10.99

Making a Civil Claim is the first law book in the *Essential Guides* series and is essential reading for anyone who has found him or herself in a dispute and who may be facing court or even a trial. It covers small claims as well as fast track and multi track cases and explains everything from organising your documents and making sure all the available evidence is in place, to finding the right solicitor or barrister for your case.

Which? Books

Other books in this series

Renting and Letting

Kate Faulkner
ISBN: 978 1 84490 029 9
Price £10.99

A practical guide for landlords, tenants, and anybody considering the buy-to-let market. Covering all the legal and financial matters, including tax, record-keeping and mortgages, as well as disputes, deposits and security, this book provides comprehensive advice for anybody involved in renting property.

Giving and Inheriting

Jonquil Lowe
ISBN: 978 1 84490 032 9
Price £10.99

Inheritance tax (IHT) is becoming a major worry for more and more people. Rising house prices have pushed up the value of typical estates to a level where they are liable to be taxed at 40% on everything over £285,000. *Giving and Inheriting* is an essential guide to estate planning and tax liability, offering up-to-the–minute advice from an acknowledged financial expert, this book will help people reduce the tax bill faced by their heirs and allow many to avoid IHT altogether.

The Pension Handbook

Jonquil Lowe
ISBN: 978 1 84490 025 1
Price £10.99

A definitive guide to sorting out your pension, whether you're deliberating over SERPs/S2Ps, organising a personal pension or moving schemes. Cutting through confusion and dispelling apathy, Jonquil Lowe provides up-to-date advice on how to maximise your savings and provide for the future.

which?

Which? Books

Which? Books

Which? Books provide impartial, expert advice on everyday matters from finance to law, property to major life events. We also publish the country's most trusted restaurant guide, *The Which? Good Food Guide*. To find out more about Which? Books, log on to www.which.co.uk or call 01903 828557.

"Which? tackles the issues that really matter to consumers and gives you the advice and active support you need to buy the right products.**"**